Lakeland Rescues Recalled

Lakeland Rescues Recalled
by Sally Bowe

First Published March 1987

ISBN No 0 902272 66 7

© Westmorland Gazette

Printed and Published by
Westmorland Gazette, Kendal, England

Contents

Contents *(Continued)*

A collection of true tales, memories after many years' active service with one of Lakeland's busiest mountain rescue teams. Not just about incidents, but about people and human emotions. Here I saw and experienced happiness, relief, fear, agony and humour. If there are lessons to be learned by others' mistakes, perhaps it may be of use to those who walk the fells today.

Lying Doggo

The attractive, blonde woman was near to tears as she told her story. "It's our dog, it's jumped off a crag in Borrowdale. It's done it before. It jumped off the cliffs at Dover and had to be rescued by the coastguard, but we can't see it and we think it might be ..... "

Three of us took the woman and her husband to the top of the crag where the dog had last been seen. It was the popular view-point of Surprise View. She told us they had been admiring the panorama when the dog suddenly launched itself out into space. "Have you been to the bottom to see?" I asked, foolishly. A look of horror spread over their faces as they gazed down the sheer hundredfoot drop. "Oh not that way," I laughed. "From the bottom road." "No," they said, "we just looked over and called."

We descended cautiously by the sheep-track that edged the crag. I called back, "What's its name?" "Bach," came the reply. "Bark?" I queried. "No, Bach, J. S. I'm a musician." "What about whistling a few bars of 'Jesu Joy of Man's desiring', muttered my colleague. We continued down and along the scree at the base of the crag. After two hours, we had found neither whisker nor bone of the missing Airedale. Puzzled, we returned to the anxious owners. "I'm sorry," I said, "there's just no sign." "Well, at least you haven't found her body," they smiled. "We'll drive up the valley, then back to Keswick. That's where we're staying."

The next day we checked with the police and the owners. There was still no sign of Bach. Determined to solve the mystery, we returned to the foot of the crag with a friend's bloodhound. Approaching the area of the previous day's search, we were disturbed to find the bloodhound pulling frantically away and to the south. "Not that way, you stupid animal," I growled. But he was determined and dragged me to the base of a neighbouring crag. Looking up, I saw, sticking out from a cleft of rock, a little face.

"It's here," I yelled, and was soon joined by my colleagues. We tethered the frantic bloodhound and climbed up to the Airedale. It was completely uninjured and though trembling violently, made no sound. Obviously, we had discovered the origin of the term "lying doggo"! The owners when presented with Bach, were ecstatic. So

pleased were they that even the bloodhound received a reward —
half a pound of minced beef. It lasted three seconds!

A coincidental sequel to the story occurred some five years later.
A tearful woman approached me, husband trailing behind. Their
dog had jumped off a crag in Borrowdale. They too had been
standing at Surprise View. To persuade the dog, this time a Cavalier
King Charles Spaniel, to leave the edge of the crag, the man had been
throwing sticks back towards the road. Unfortunately, in so doing,
he had kicked another stick down over the edge. That, of course, was
the stick the animal chose to retrieve!

"We'll find it," I boasted rashly. Half-an-hour later, having
abseiled from the view-point, my conviction began to fade. At this
point I came eye-to-eye with the spaniel. Like Bach, he too was
uninjured and mute and was returned to grateful owners. We
decided there must be something in the air at Surprise View that
encouraged dogs into sky-diving!

Wet on Wythburn Ghyll

The sergeant on duty at Keswick police station wearily reached for pencil and paper. A caller had reported the loss of "one of his boys." His story unfolds slowly and eventually the sergeant telephones the local mountain rescue team leader to explain, "we've got a teacher here. He's been up Wythburn Ghyll with twenty boys and he's lost one somewhere." The rescue team responds rapidly to a call-out and within ten minutes two truck-loads are leaving the rescue Headquarters. One group is to search from Stonethwaite, in the Borrowdale Valley, towards Greenup; the second search from Steel End, Thirlmere up Wythburn Ghyll to rendezvous on the summit ridge.

The wind-screen wipers work overtime. It has been raining continuously for two days, the becks are white and foaming. At Steel End, the team pile out into the farmyard. "Now, me lads, wat's oop?" the farmer shouts from the shelter of the barn-door. His jacket-collar is turned up and he wears his cap. It must be wet! He is told briefly and his comments typify local attitudes: "They want nowt up there on a day like this."

The men trudge up towards the fell-gate. Water is running down the track and great stretches of bog have formed. Searchers split up into ones and twos. Several attempt to cross the beck to travel up the far bank. They end up wading, fatalistically realising that they are going to get wet anyway. By now, rain is trickling in at the neck and working its way into the boots, preparing to travel up the stockings. Radio contact has already been lost with Keswick base and as yet, they are not in contact with the second party travelling up from Stonethwaite.

"When did he last see this lad?" a team member shouts. The question is relayed to the teacher and accompanying searcher, by now trailing well behind the main group. "He doesn't know," comes the reply.

An hour passes, the rain continues, the rescuers progress uphill. By now they are sweating with their exertions, and water has trickled under their waterproofs. They are wet from inside and out, they are hot and hungry. It is almost tea-time and the daylight is fading. The teacher has been taken back to the farm, tired and wet. The rescuers carry on, because somewhere up here is a young boy, lost, cold, tired and hungry. He did not ask to be taken fell-walking in the rain, and he'll probably never want to come again.

Now both groups of searchers are in low cloud at about fourteen hundred feet. "How do you find anyone in this?" "You fall over them," was the experienced answer. Half-an-hour later there comes a shout, "He's here!" The thirteen-year-old is near to tears and panic-stricken. "It's O.K., son, we'll soon have you down." Personal discomfort is forgotten as sympathy is extended to the boy. Relief and elation at success restore morale among the rescuers. The boy is capable of walking down and there is a light-hearted atmosphere as most return to the farm. A group of three have to carry on to the ridge to establish radio contact with the Borrowdale party and Keswick base. Their pace is fast, the job almost finished. Arriving on the ridge, the call is put out. "K2 to K3 over." When contact is made, the message is transmitted, "The boy has been found safe and well. Return to base. Out."

Blown to bits

I thrust my feet into climbing boots and ran towards the road. I'd been canoeing with a group on the lake when the first truck-load of rescuers had passed. I knew I'd be in time for the second vehicle. Sure enough, within minutes, I heard the horns sounding and the Land-Rover halted as the driver saw me. I jumped into the back and we set off down the valley. The call was to a rock-climber, who had severe head injuries. Everyone knew this was urgent.

When we arrived at the farm-yard, the equipment was quickly apportioned and we followed the first group of team-members. The climb was a steep, thousand feet of fell-side and our pace was fast. Fell-walkers stopped to watch as we puffed past them. The radio crackled into life. "Don't rush, lads. There's no need to hurry now." We understood the concealed message. We were not now rescuing a severely injured casualty. We were recovering a body. We slowed down to a more comfortable rate. The stretcher suddenly felt heavy on my shoulders and I was aware that I was damp with the drizzle that was falling.

The radio called again. "Second party, intercept the climber who was with this chap. He's coming down the track towards you. He doesn't know." I looked up. A tall young man was heading downhill towards us. He was carrying climbing equipment and two rucksacks. I called to him, he came across and we gave him the news.

I pass the stretcher to another team-member and go down to the farmhouse with the young man. He starts to talk. "We'd finished climbing and were having coffee. It was too wet to do anything serious. I looked around and he was soloing the slab. Suddenly he just slipped. I ran down to the foot of the crag but his face was badly injured. I thought he was .....". I talked to him, trying to console him, but what should one say to a bloke who has just lost his best friend?

At the farm, the police were waiting. I handed him over gratefully, relieved from embarrassment. I knew he had to make a statement for the coroner and give all personal details. I wandered back to the vehicle. The body was just being brought down and the equipment being returned. Three of us drove to the mortuary and unloaded.

Then we all went back to work. My group had left the lake and were drying out at the centre.

Five days later the police 'phoned my home. Would I be free to take some policemen up to the scene of the accident? I agreed, without surprise. This often happened. I met them at the farm and as we travelled up to the crag, they questioned me — just the usual questions: How far had he fallen? How did his mate react? Did he want to see the body? We accomplished the last part of the journey in silence.

At their request, I pointed to the foot of the crag where we had found the body. I realised they were looking for something and had found some coins. After about twenty minutes' search, both at the foot and on the crag, they returned, shaking their heads. "What's the matter?" I asked, puzzled. "It's like this," one said. "Only one thing is missing from the body, and that's his wedding ring." "They often pull off when a body falls," I replied. "Yes, but when that happens you can see marks of violence on the finger. We think his wedding ring was removed." Still puzzled, I pressed on. "Why?" They looked at each other. "We suspect this bloke has gone off with the dead man's wife." "You're kidding!" I said. I realised that they weren't.

The town was rife with the gossip when I returned. News travels fast in small towns like Keswick. Speculation grew as days passed, but days lengthened into weeks, weeks into months. When nothing further was heard, the short-memoried found hotter stories to discuss.

Twelve months later, I was stopped in town by a local policeman. "Remember that bloke, his mate was killed on the crag and he ran off with the missus?" "Aye." "Well, he's deed. He was blown to bits by a shot-gun." His own wife was paralysed, in a wheel-chair and she had this male nurse. Well, he twigged what was up, followed matie around, caught up with him in Devon and shot him. It's in this morning's paper. He's been committed to Broadmoor."

Too heavy

I jumped aboard the already moving vehicle, bound for Jenkin Hill, Skiddaw "What is it?" "Broken ankle." Good, I thought, short trip, short, sharp pull up the fell and injury not too bad."

It was one of those days when the tourist traffic was at its silliest and slowest. A mini-van full of sightseers was following us, too closely. One of our police team members leaned forward, in full view through the rear of our vehicle and slowly replaced his helmet. The mini-van dropped back. People waved as we passed by, making us feel like competitors in a rally. As we turned up the Gale Road, we met a car head-on in the centre of the narrow lane. He panicked, seeing the blue light and was unable to find reverse-gear immediately. After several attempts, he managed to pull half off the road, on our side. We waved thank-you and continued.

At the top, where the road finished, we turned off into the field. Then it was foot-slogging, carrying two stretcher-halves, sleeping-bags and covers, first-aid and ropes. Panting, we overtook several walkers. They thought we were super-fit! Our lungs and hearts told us we were not, merely pushing ourselves to the limit. At Half-way House, the non-existent cafe, we got our second wind. We lifted our eyes from the ground and thankfully saw a small group standing above. Lying at their feet was a short, plump woman. I stared in disbelief. She was wearing Scholl's sandals! I smiled sympathetically, still out of breath. "This is the last time I come climbing," she moaned. "I didn't want to come anyway and now I've broken my leg."

We zipped an inflatable splint on to her leg and lifted her, with some difficulty, on to the stretcher. "I'm on a diet," she said. "Just relax," I soothed. "We're just going to sledge you down to the ambulance."

It took six of us to lift her over the barbed-wire fence to the waiting Land-Rover ambulance. We loaded her in, reassured her and drove carefully towards the only track through the marshy field. We miscalculated, just slightly and sank. "We've got a little wheel-spin," we told her, as we jumped out with shovels. "I knew I was too heavy," she wailed. "Not at all, not at all," we said, frantically signalling to the other vehicle to come and tow us out. In rescuing us, the second truck put himself in jeopardy and stuck. But, we were free and continued down on the understanding we would return if he had not extricated himself by the time we had the patient in hospital. Fortunately, all ended well. The casualty was X-rayed, plastered and returned to her relatives. Both Land-Rovers were garaged, whole and entire, within a few hours.

Wet and Smelly

We arrive in Rosthwaite and a group of little boys playing in the farmyard shout across to us, "They're up there," We see where they're pointing and set off carrying the gear. As we cross the stepping-stones, I think to myself, "I wonder who'll be walking through this beck on the way down."

Two fields later, an amazing sight greets our eyes. At least fifteen women are standing around, chattering animatedly. In the centre of the group, also smiling and chatting, a man is lying. One of his boots has been removed and another man is photographing him. A Great Dane, attached to one of the women, is the only member of the party looking concerned. He eyes us suspiciously. The man lying on the ground, possibly the casualty, notices us. "Hello, chaps. Sorry about all this. Bit of bad luck you know. I was minding my own business when this damned rock appeared in the bracken and the next I knew I was lying here and all those lovely creatures were examining me. They're nurses on a fell walk."

We kneel down and look at his ankle. It is very swollen but when we touch him the dog growls menacingly. "Alfie!" barks the casualty. "Down, sir!" The woman attached to Alfie's lead tries valiantly to hold him still. "Pan in on this, Godfrey. Get some good shots of this. It might be the only opportunity ever. Not that I'm not grateful to you chaps, but we must record it, mustn't we?" The other man photographs the splinting and stretchering routine, the women chattered and Alfie begins to cry. "Quiet, sir, quiet!" shouts our casualty.

We try to tell him what we are going to do, but we can't get a word in for his monologue. We start the carry-down. "What a week this has been. I run a club in the North-East. We do boxing and fell-walking. On Monday a bulldozer demolished the boxing-club by mistake, supposed to be knocking down the church next door. Today, we hired a coach to come walking. We got half-way up Honister Pass when it developed brake trouble. We had to reverse down again. So the driver's waiting for a replacement and we came up here. Now this thing's happened. I say, what time is it?" "Twelve-thirty" I manage to interpose. Alfie is pushing me, in an attempt to get nearer to his master. "Twelve-thirty, the pub's still open. I'd like to get you chaps a drink. Do we have time?" We point out that perhaps the local landlord wouldn't take too kindly to a stretcher being propped up against his bar. "Well, perhaps after the hospital," he says. "I'm extremely indebted to you."

We have reached the beck. Alfie is still pushing and I am one of those who paddle across knee-deep. When we load our patient into the Land-Rover ambulance, Alfie frantically pushes in. "Good boy, good boy, down, sir," bellows the casualty. None of us can persuade Alfie to get out and he travels to Keswick in great comfort, sitting on my lap! He is wet and smelly. So am I. We unload our man on to the X-ray table. "Thanks so much, chaps. Must keep in touch. Cheerie-bye." We head back to Headquarters, unload, tidy, clean and re-pack. The 'phone rings. It's the police station telling us a lad has fallen off Shepherd's Crag, Black Icicle. We jump in and again race off down Borrowdale. The young man does not seem too seriously injured, despite the fact that he is not wearing a climbing helmet. We take him to hospital.

As we carry him in we notice a coach in the car-park. It is full of tourists and our earlier casualty is hobbling out to it, plastered to the knee. "Not again, chaps," he shouts. "Good show." Nurses push him and Alfie on board. Everyone waves goodbye. We return to the H.Q. and for the second time that day we tidy, clean and re-load the equipment. I get into my car and head out, past the hospital and on to the A66. A figure in uniform is walking down towards Keswick. I notice a coach stopped on the road-side. This is the driver. Our friend's replacement coach has also broken down! I take him to the telephone and then run him back to his vehicle. "Good show!" I hear, echoing from its interior. When I return two hours later, they have all gone. I learned later that they reached home without further mishap. But it had been quite a day!

Helicopter rescue

On what my companion judged "a grand day" we struggled up from Stockley Bridge. We pushed on, looking admiringly at the afternoon sun reflecting on the snow-covered tops. Effort prevented much conversation as we headed for Great End up Grains Ghyll. Our pace did not slacken until we reached the white bridge. Here we had to pause for a staggered crossing. Its narrowness meant crossing singly, at the same time lifting one's rucksack to avoid its catching on the high wooden sides.

There was thick, grey ice where the sun had not reached. Although we felt warm in the sun, a light breeze made us shiver as we waited. "Cold day for lying around," I said, thinking of our casualty. The only information we had was that he had fallen down Great End and was badly injured. That could mean anything, but we knew we had to hurry. We had taken the precaution of putting an Air-Sea Rescue helicopter on standby. We were able to call upon Sea-Kings from RAF Boulmer in Northumberland. An unnecessary call meant a lot of wasted money, so we always made sure its flight was needed before enlisting its help.

As we crossed Ruddy Ghyll we looked up to the massive bulk of Great End, plastered with thick snow. A waving hand alerted us, and we made out a small group standing on the plateau, a good distance from the crag itself. The snow here was soft and impeded our progress as we crossed. A quick examination of our conscious casualty revealed multiple injuries, including, our priority, a severe head wound. I gave the signal to have the helicopter called and we gently treated our patient and got him on to the stretcher.

We explained to him that we had sent for a helicopter as it was getting late in the day and that a traditional carried recovery would be overtaken by darkness. A casualty is easily alarmed by the idea and noise of a helicopter. We thought he had understood, but we were aware he was drifting into a semi-conscious state.

While we waited, his friends explained what had happened. The three of them came climbing every Wednesday afternoon. Today they had been climbing in Cust's Gully. Conditions were good and they had had an enjoyable day. The casualty had been leading and was just stepping out at the top when he had turned, slipped and fallen the whole way down again. We estimated he had fallen at least 800 feet!

"Here it is!" came a call. We turned in surprise, to see a tiny, yellow spot, coming up the valley towards us. To my amazement it had taken half-an-hour. We learned later that they had left shortly after our first call, thinking that it was a nice day for a trip to the Lake District! It was fortunate, though, for our casualty. The noise grew louder and we saw the snow disturbed by the rotors. Three of us leaned over the stretcher to protect our man from the blizzard that had been whipped up. As it landed we were soaked and deafened. The crew-man waved us over and we sledged the stretcher and kept low. We lifted the patient on board and two of us accompanied him.

Within minutes we were airborne and heading towards Whitehaven. A magnificent sunset appeared over the Solway, but we hardly had time to appreciate it before we were landing on the hospital heli-pad. We were evidently unexpected or early, because no ambulance was waiting. We unloaded the stretcher and headed towards the building. It was a long way through the corridors to Casualty Department. Here we took our casualty into a sideward and left him in capable hands.

As we returned to the helicopter we were aware of our incongruity. Patients and staff stared as two mountaineers and a helicopter crew-man clattered along those scrupulously clean corridors in boots and heavy, outdoor clothing. We were delighted to find that our air-taxi had been doubly useful: they had collected some recently donated kidneys to fly back to Newcastle. We were dropped back in Keswick before the sun had disappeared, marvelling at the speed of the whole incident. Our casualty made a rapid recovery and survived to continue climbing each Wednesday for many years.

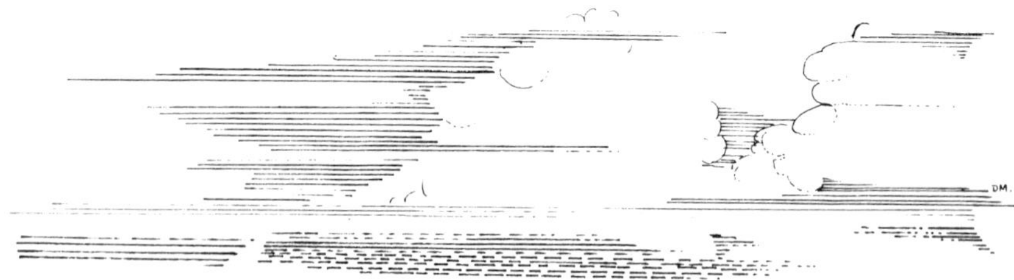

Walking and snoring

At half-past-six, the 'phone rang and by quarter-to-seven a truck-load of men were leaving Keswick and heading down Borrowdale towards Seathwaite. The farmer was waiting for us. "It's a lady on Allen Crags," he said. "It's likely going to rain," he added as we set off. "Job's comforter," we retorted. We took a shortcut over the shoulder from Grains Ghyll, up the steep sides of Allen Crags. We remembered the farmer's warning as the first few spots of rain began to fall with the dusk. We found three elderly folk near the summit. "We're so pleased to see you," said an old lady of seventy-six. "We'd done Scafell Pike and we thought we'd just do Glaramara, too, when she slipped and broke her ankle. We're all very cold. We had to wait ages before anyone came along and he didn't know the way to Seathwaite very well." We did a quick assessment of the situation and decided we had two stretcher cases. Besides the woman with the broken leg there was an elderly man who was showing the first stages of exposure. We loaded them on to the stretchers and took the decision to walk the second lady, of the trio rather than wait for another stretcher to be brought. By now it was dark, cold and wet. All our personnel were assisting with the carry, and there was no-one to do the route-finding. We did not realise the stupidity of this until we began to descend rapidly at a point where we felt we should not be doing so. Already we were committed. There was no alternative but to continue.

Our walking casualty was snoring. It was the first time I had seen someone walking and sleeping at the same time. By now we were more or less carrying her. We were all soaked to the skin and unable to use our torches as we had no free hands. We knew something had gone wrong but were unable to establish what until we heard someone say, "Angle Tarn." Then we understood what had happened. We had taken the wrong side of the fell. Instead of returning to Grains Ghyll and the comfort of Seathwaite, we had come down near Angle Tarn and now had to face the seemingly endless trudge down Kangstrath to Stonethwaite.

The two casualties on the stretchers were protected from the weather and quite comfortable but we were worried about our

"Sleeping Beauty"! Still she seemed to have tremendous willpower and reserves of strength. In her waking moments she regaled us with stories of her life and about her pet budgie, and at one point she even burst into song. I prayed that she wasn't delirious!

At three a.m., the lights of Stonethwaite appeared. With great relief we saw the waiting ambulance and loaded our three sleeping casualties. "There's coffee in the hotel," someone said. I went inside. "Great," I said to the chap who handed me a cup. "Kind of the landlord." "He doesn't know," he said. "I found the door open and went into the kitchen." As we were laughing, a bedroom door opened and a man appeared in a dressing-gown. He contemplated the group standing in his hall, laughing and drinking his coffee at three in the morning, shook his head, turned, and went back to bed. Obviously he thought he was dreaming. The next day, having explained, we tried to reimburse him. He refused. Typical of the sort of kindness we were so often shown. We had learned a lesson, though. Our casualties had suffered no ill-effects, but no thanks to us! Our organisation and planning were much more careful ever after.

Mine Rescue

When I arrived at the headquarters extra equipment was being loaded unhurriedly into the back of the Land-Rover. Metal poles, hammers, shovels and lights gradually filled the floor space. "What on earth is it?" I queried. "Mine-rescue at Caldbeck, but it's O.K. They've sent for the special mine-rescue squad." "What special mine-rescue squad and where's it coming from?" I puzzled. The reply was that the "police have it in hand." I sensed some confusion and pausing only to enlist the help of a few local ex-miners, we headed for the back of Skiddaw.

At the ford, we were stopped by a police car. The constable gave us further instructions and we turned up the mine-road. It was a warm, sunny evening and about five o'clock. Ahead, we saw two high-ranking police officers, sweating along in dazzlingly white shirts. We offered them a lift, which they gladly accepted.

The story came to light as we bounced along the pitted track. At midday, a man from Carlisle had entered the mine searching for geological specimens. In his excitement at finding a particularly fine piece of campalite, he accidentally kicked the roof-support. These mines had been disused for about seventy years and were known to be dangerous. His action had brought down the roof. He had been totally buried. Fortunately, his young son, waiting on the surface, had heard the noise of falling rock and had run for help. A local farmer had found him in great distress. Two other geologists and specimen hunters who were staying at his farm rushed to help.

Not thinking of their own safety and fully aware of the danger these two men had climbed down to the casualty and managed to clear his face so that he was able to breathe. Meanwhile, the farmer had alerted the police. The area was a divisional boundary and there was a slight problem about which police section should deal with the problem. It was by then two o'clock.

Eventually Wigton police accepted the responsibility and began to ask for additional civilian aid. They had called out the special mine-rescue unit from Ambleside, the NCB mine-rescue squad from Workington, the fire brigade, an RAF helicopter from Boulmer and our rescue team.

When we arrived at the location all we saw were half-a-dozen policemen, two civilians and a nasty-looking hole in the ground. It was about three feet square and set in loose shale in the bottom of what resembled a mine-dumping. We all stopped. It was worse than we feared. The whole area was obviously moving and treacherous. "Well, someone will have to go down," I said, reaching for a helmet. "There's only room for about two," one of the geologists warned, "and the air gets pretty foul." We remembered a recent cave-rescue where the rescuers had "drowned" their casualty in their own expired air.

We erected the metal mine-poles which enabled us to span the entrance hole and dropped a rope down, without having to touch the crumbling sides. Cautiously, I dropped the twelve vertical feet into the tunnel. Then I walked down towards a chamber. It was blocked at the far end and there I saw a man's head sticking up through the floor. There was a beam above his head and I guessed that this supported the whole roof of rock-debris. I lay down and crawled the last few feet to talk to him. He was conscious and lucid. "For God's sake, get me out," he pleaded. "O.K. But it's not going to be easy," I told him, trying to sound calm. I began picking pieces of rock from around his head and passing them to the other rescuer behind me. That was how it went on, picking one piece after another, for five hours. There was not room to work a shovel nor, when it came to moving the beam of wood, a saw. We used the bare saw-blade, wrapped in rags. All the time we talked to reassure the casualty —trivialities about his wife and family and about geology. All the time, we kept checking that the beam of wood was not moving. I had planned to back rapidly up the passage if it started to move. I knew that probably I would not reach the entrance hole. We sweated, with exertion and with fear.

A shout alerted us. Radios don't work underground. A doctor had arrived and was on his way down. He was not young but very reassuring. He examined what he could see of the man and gave him an injection. "Just enough to calm him down," he said. "Not enough to put him out, you'll need his help later." "Do you think we could have one?" we joked. He smiled wryly and returned to the surface.

Here there was a seething mass of inertia. The fire engine and crew had arrived, so had three Land-Rovers with the mine-rescue unit, and the NCB rescue vehicle. The helicopter was just approaching. They were all powerless, able only to stand by. Underground, the sound of the helicopter landing was magnified, almost unbearably.

Thinking it was another rock-fall, our casualty gritted his teeth and we all prayed. "Don't worry," I shouted, "It's miles away. It only sounds like on top." He said something unprintable. We carried on lifting piece after piece and passing it back.

Gradually, we got his arms free. He appeared uninjured. "There's nothing under my feet," he said. "Right," I said, "we're going to pull." I grasped him under the armpits, my colleague seized my ankles and we heaved. He screamed. "Come on," I urged, "You'll soon be free." We pulled again. He began to come free. I scraped a few more rocks from around him and managed to drag him back up into the tunnel. The roof had stayed intact. We breathed sighs of relief.

We shouted for a stretcher, which was passed down to us. We strapped him on and sledged him to the entrance-hole. The doctor was waiting to check him again and hurriedly wrote a letter to accompany him on his helicopter flight to hospital where he was found to have no injuries at all. We staggered home to remove five hours of mine dirt in a hot shower and replace the considerable amount of fluid we had lost!

It's these damned wellies

Wolf Crags was our destination one sunny winter's afternoon. They stand on the Old Coach Road between Dockray and Threlkeld, but I didn't know anyone ever went there. The rescue call had come from one of the isolated farm houses on Troutbeck Common and that was where we found ourselves some half-an-hour later. The farmer stood waiting for us at the door. "You'll not get the vehicle along the road," he said. "It's been blocked with snow since last Monday. I'll show you the way up the beck."

We set off, but not at our usual pace. The snow was deep and we had to lift our feet at every step. Although it was only four o'clock, the sun was setting, the snow flushed with its scarlet rays. Once in shadow, the intense cold was felt even through our exertions. The farmer was well ahead, almost as though he did not want to talk to us. We thought this strange: these farmers are usually extremely talkative and friendly. We hurried after him as best we could. His dogs ran between us, excitedly wagging their tails and panting.

After three-quarters of an hour we reached the foot of the crag. "This is where I stop," he announced, pointing upwards. "He's there." "Who?" we queried. "My friend from yon farm. He's not hurt, just stuck. It's his wellies. Like mine, slape." We looked upwards and could make out the figure of a man about fifty feet above us. He was facing the crag, but half-turned and gave us a wave. "I'se areet," he shouted, "but I can't get doon."

We took the precaution of fitting instep-crampons before walking up to him with a rope. "I'm gay sorry to bring you lads out. It's these damned wellies. I can move neither up nor down. I was shepherding and two yows ran up here. I followed them in case they got stuck and before I realised it, I was committed. Don't know why I didn't put me boots on," he apologised. We tied him on to the rope and fixed it to a belay. Then we gently lowered and slithered him to the base of the crag. "I feel that foolish," he said. "I bet you feel a bit cold, too," I said. "How long had you been there?" "About two hours, but I'se not cold. Good job I had me flask of peach-brandy in me pocket. I'm sorry I've none left!"

As we drove him back to the village he was still apologising and thanking us. He shifted awkwardly as we approached his home. "Look lads, would you mind dropping me here? I don't want anyone to see me getting out of your vehicle. The missus will kill me." Sensitive to his embarrassment, we stopped short of his back door and let him out. "By the way," I said, "what happened to the ewes you followed?" "Oh, they waited till I was stuck and then ran away safe and sound."

I've found them

It was New Year's Day. Dense, low cloud hung over the fells and it was damp and dismal. Those suffering from the excesses of the night before felt justified in staying quietly at home. But the call came and the search-dogs were turned out. The story was a little vague. Two local boys were spending the holiday walking and hostelling. They had failed to turn up at a youth hostel in Borrowdale but, as they were well-equipped no-one was over-concerned. All the same, because the weather was poor it was decided to do a token search.

Their route was not known in detail. They were presumed possibly missing in an area between Eskdale and Borrowdale. This is a large area in which many routes exist. Because the weather of the previous few days had not been clear a further presumption was made: that the youths would not have tackled any high peaks. It was also felt that the boys might have checked in at a hostel or guest house elsewhere. The police were working along those lines. The next day, after negative results, a full-scale, multi-team search was planned. The day dawned brilliantly clear with the snow-covered tops shining silver against the deep blue sky. There was warmth in the sun. It was a day to be out and about, one that made you feel glad to be alive.

A small group of us made our way up from Seathwaite to Styhead Tarn. Other parties were covering Grains Ghyll, Langstrath, Wasdale and Eskdale. Our job was to search the area of crags above and below the Corridor Route to Scafell Pike. This is a notorious black-spot where it is easy to lose the way. Already there were fell-walkers out on the tops. This was the sort of day that the holidaymakers waited for and made their holiday worthwhile.

A helicopter appeared above the Tarn and turned up towards Scafell Pike. "Good flying day," someone said. "He's doing more than that," I said. "He's actually dropping men and dogs at various high points so they can search down-hill." "However did we manage without choppers?" someone else asked. As we approached Lingmell Col we heard an excited radio message. "I've found them!" We stopped to listen as the radio procedure became more formalised. We learned that a man and his dog had been dropped on the summit of Scafell Pike. When the helicopter had left he had walked around the cairn and discovered the two bodies. A slight complication now arose. A strong wind had got up and the helicopter was unable to return.

Another radio message came through. "We are in Lingmell Col with a stretcher and will be on the summit within twenty minutes." We looked around, puzzled and then noticed a small group moving up out of Hollow Stones. We joined them and together shared the carry of the stretcher to the summit. The bodies of the two boys lay close to the summit-cairn. Their rucksacks were next to them. They contained warm clothing and waterproofs. We presumed that the lads, tired by their efforts climbing and fighting bad weather conditions, had sat down and quietly drifted into sleep. Hypothermia is insidious, overcoming before symptoms are recognised. We stood silent in the sharp brilliance of that winter's day.

Our thoughts were interrupted by the throb of the returning helicopter. "It's too windy. He'll never land," someone predicted. The aircraft hovered above Mickledore, then drifted sideways in the strong wind towards us. It landed on one wheel, tilted, counteracting the gusts. Its rotor-blades seemed very close to the summit cairn. A second stretcher was almost thrown out and simultaneously the helicopter lifted off again. The winch-man signalled that it was impossible to stay. We undertook a traditional carry. Already the first tourists were arriving on the summit, pleased at their successful conquest and with the beauty of this perfect winter's day.

The 'sack was empty

The farmer's wife was worried. Three days before, a woman in a red anorak with a Sheltie dog had walked through the farm-yard with a small child — a "la'al babby" — on her back in a rucksack. "I saw its little flaxen head. It was just about the same age as our little grandson, that's why I noticed it. That was at mid-day. I saw her come back about five o'clock and she didn't have that baby with her. The 'sack was empty." Sensing her concern, I promised to tell the police, although all that was Wednesday and now it was Saturday.

Within the hour, a Task Force had been drafted in to make enquiries at local hotels and guesthouses. We ourselves were asked to assess the distance a woman could travel from Seathwaite within the time-span indicated by the farmer's wife. We then had to search these areas looking for the body of a baby. We drove down Borrowdale speculating on where we would hide a body. It was not an attractive day's outing. I looked gloomily through the window. We were passing through Rosthwaite. On the footpath I noticed a young couple. The woman wore a red anorak and carried a baby. The man had a Sheltie dog on a lead. "Stop!" I shouted. We screeched to a halt and I leapt out. My colleagues stared, amazed at my strange behaviour.

I ran back to the couple and stopped dead. What could I say? "Excuse me." I looked at the woman. "Did you go for a walk on Wednesday?" She glanced at her husband, "Er, yes." "Did you take the baby with you, at about midday?" "Yes." "Did you come back at about five o'clock without the baby?" "Yes." What else could I ask? I paused and saw the baby. "Is this the baby?" "Yes." "But what's the matter?" "The police are looking for you." "What do you mean?" she questioned, thoroughly alarmed. "Well, because you came back without the baby. The farmer's wife was worried about it." The young man burst out laughing. "That's easy to explain. My wife and I are both keen walkers. Since we've had the baby it's been more difficult to get out. Last Wednesday I went out in the morning and my wife stayed back to look after him. At midday she brought him and a packed lunch and we met at Stockley Bridge. After we ate she went for a walk and I brought the baby back. When she came back at five the baby and I were waiting for her in the car."

Relieved, I radioed the message back to base and the police station. We were ordered to take the couple and the baby down to Seathwaite. Here the wife was asked to perform a reconstruction. With the baby in her rucksack she marched up and down the farmyard. The farmer's wife made a positive identification and we all adjourned to the farmhouse for tea and cake. A bizarre situation had reached a satisfactory conclusion.

Walking in circles

It was a warm summer's night as we turned into the farmyard. A tearful woman was sitting in the house. The farmer's wife was consoling her. "Poor soul," she told us. "She was just sitting in the car, crying her eyes out." The story unfolded. Her husband had left her for a walk at ten a.m. She had expected him back by two. At four she was found weeping and now, at nine, he had still not returned. We told her not to worry. It was warm and light and he'd probably just missed the track. In answer to our questions she told us he had no map, no local knowledge, no spare clothing, no torch, no survival bag and no walking experience!

We set off for Styhead Tarn. The evening was absolutely still and peaceful. "I bet he could hear us on the Pike if we shouted," we joked. We shouted his name together and were surprised to hear a reply. "Where are you?" we shouted again. "Here," came the reply. "Great," we laughed. "Where the heck is that? Say again," we shouted. "Here, here, here," came the voice. "Sounds like the Corridor Route," I said. We trudged up through the silent night. By eleven o'clock it was barely dark but we were well on the way to Lingmell Col. Further shouting had brought no response so we presumed we were in an unfavourable position. "He can't have been this far away," I said. "Let's give another holler." We bellowed again. The reply came from behind us. "We've passed him," we sighed.

We retraced our route and eventually located him below the track on rough ground. He was exhausted and very pleased to see us. "I must have been walking in circles for hours," he said. We sat down and had a flask of coffee. He told us his tale. It had been a lovely day and he had had no trouble getting to the summit of Scafell Pike. But he'd stayed there longer than he'd intended and when he'd left there was no-one else on the track for him to follow. He had apparently dropped down into Broad Crag Col and turned left, got into Lingmell Col and returned to the summit again. He recognised his mistake and arriving in Broad Crag Col for a second time had turned sharp right and found himself on the summit again! This time he had dropped into Lingmell Col and eventually found himself standing by a very big cairn. We presumed this to be Lingmell. He had then walked down the front of Lingmell into a steep ravine. We gasped! This was obviously Piers Ghyll. He had climbed out of this ravine and been wandering about ever since.

Our progress down was slow as the poor chap barely had the strength to lift his feet. He was carrying a shopping basket containing what was left of his meal. I wondered how on earth he'd managed to climb out of Piers Ghyll with a shopping basket in his hands. Perhaps he'd carried it in his teeth.

At three o'clock, the sky began to lighten. "Not far now," we urged as he dragged his unwilling limbs down the track. We hoped his wife didn't intend shouting at him in feminine fury. Mercifully, she did no such thing. Instead she flung her arms around him in delight. He staggered under the force of her enthusiasm and smiled weakly. Once again, the farmer's wife triumphed with hot tea all round and a warm bed for the weary wanderer. We made our way back to Keswick in daylight ready for a few hours sleep before work.

He's eighty-nine

A holidaymaker asked me if I'd lost my dog. "Sort of," I said, "but it's the man who's attached to it that we're more concerned about." It wasn't that he was unfamiliar with the fells. He had founded the rescue team nineteen years before and had been a mountaineer all his life. But now, he was eighty-nine and had little sense of time. He had gone up Skiddaw three hours before to see the fell-race. He hadn't returned.

It had been a long day and we told the tale to the interested tourist. The hottest summer in living memory had produced a scorching Sunday, when more than a hundred fell-runners raced the nine mountain-miles from Keswick and over Skiddaw summit. As we stood watching the ascent, we pitied the runners. "It's too hot, should have been abandoned," frowned one of the senior team members. It was not, though, until the runners returned past our radio post that we realised the significance of his words. Men with glazed expressions poured the cups of drinking-water over their heads. There was none of the cheerful banter as some staggered and lurched silently like drunken men. "Look at these three!" the onlookers gasped. Three ran abreast, the two on the outside buttressing their semi-conscious colleague between. "They're after the team prize," I said. "If they let him retire, they lose. It's insane." Hearing a shout we turned. One man had reached us, totally disorientated and had started back up again. He was fielded by other runners and pointed downhill.

Two hours after the start of the race the last runner arrived back and the full score was known. Twenty-five runners had needed emergency treatment for exhaustion, including fluid replacement, in the local hospital. Miraculously only two were detained and they were discharged the next day, after a good night's sleep. Now our problem was the missing president, a wiry character from an age when a day on the fells meant cycling from Penrith to Borrowdale, walking up to Gable and rock-climbing all day, returning by the same route. A career as an officer in the Army toughened him further and bushwhacking in Canada developed his independent spirit. At seventy, as he was unable to find an insurance company to take him on for ski-ing holidays in the Alps, he travelled to Norway where insurance was not needed. To him, Skiddaw was an afternoon's stroll.

Three of us wearily climbed Jenkin Hill for the third time that day. In the distance, a movement was discernible. The binoculars confirmed it was the old man returning. We hailed him as he approached. "This damned dog's had me through a bog," he complained. "Won't do a thing I tell it, undisciplined. I'll tell its owner when I get back, needs to go to obedience classes." He descended rapidly, the old soldier leading his men. We bundled them into the Land-Rover and took them home. "Here, hold the dog for me while I hose it down," he ordered. His failing eyesight was his only concession to the ageing process. "The dog's still bone-dry and I'm soaked," I complained. "Give me the hose and you hold the dog."

His wife appeared at the door, a frail seventy-year old. He reflected: "Look at her. Here am I, twenty years her senior, with all my faculties and poor old thing she's almost senile. On my nintieth birthday next year I'm going to climb Napes Needle in the afternoon and have a good meal and booze-up in the evening. I'll invite that nice young lady doctor." His eyes twinkled. "Thanks for the ride." He disappeared inside, leaving me holding the bedraggled spaniel. The owner eyed me suspiciously when I told him it had fallen into a tarn. No longer caring, suddenly weary, I headed for home.

I'm that clown in the white sweater

We gazed at the gully and just waited for an accident to happen. We had been up Scafell Pike and had no wish to go all the way back to Keswick only to turn round to pick up these blokes. Four people were visible in the gully on the far side of the ravine from where we were standing. They were climbing in a direct line in a gully full of loose scree and rock. It was fairly obvious from our viewpoint that it was only a matter of time before one or other of them kicked a rock down on to his colleague or colleagues below. Chance would determine the outcome.

We waited for half-an-hour. Then there was activity opposite. Two had climbed back down to the third. Ten minutes later, one in a white pullover climbed out of the gully on to the rock at the side. "They're abandoning the gully," I said. "Must have had enough," my companion decided.

We set off down to Seathwaite. The farmer was in the barn. "Noo, me lads," he greeted us. "What's thoo been up till?" We told him our story and chatted about sheep and the weather. We took our leave as a young man came to talk to him. The farmer called us back. "There's been an accident on Base Brown. This lad wants a rescue team." "It's not that clown in the white sweater, is it?" I asked in amazement. "I'm that clown in the white sweater," said the young man huffily, overhearing my comment. "I took it off because it was hot." "We've been watching you for ages waiting for the accident," I told him. "Don't be stupid," he retorted, "There's nothing dangerous about that gully." "It's rotten," I replied. "Well, Wainwright says it's perfectly safe and recommends it as an ascent route," he said. Unable to question that, we gathered the stretcher and other items of equipment and set off, back up the fell.

When we reached the casualty, we found that the full extent of his injury amounted to a cut on the hand. "Lucky it wasn't his head. No hats in a spot like this!" whispered someone. "It's perfectly safe according to the lad who raised the alarm. He reckons Wainwright says it's okay," I said. "Never!" was the incredulous reply. I promised to look it up when we got back. All rescue teams have a full set of Wainwright's Lakeland Guides. They give more immediate and detailed information than a map, particularly when in unfamiliar territory. They have proved invaluable on many occasions.

We brought our casualty down and insisted that he visited hospital, despite his protests. We hurried back to headquarters and tidied away. At last, I reached for Wainwright's Western Fells. Triumphantly, I exonerated Wainwright and read aloud:

"It is not listed as a rock-climb, either because it is too easy or too impossible. It is certain to be dangerous."

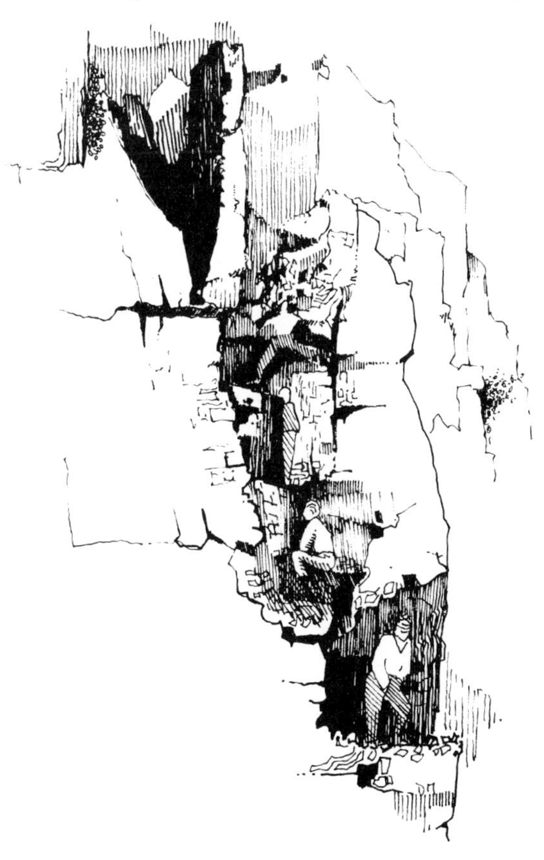

Four casualties

In our capacity as mountain rescuers, we had been employed to oversee the navigation of a group of young Army officers in the Scafells. Once above 1500 feet the cloud descended, leaving us all in that thick, gloomy, grey mist which merged with the porridgy snow, producing a condition known as a white-out. We trudged on for another while, then the two officers leading halted for a rapid discussion. Shamefacedly, they approached us. "We're not too sure of our position actually," one of them started. "Do you think it would be wise, in these weather conditions, to return to base?" "Yes, probably the sensible thing to do," we bluffed. "Just retrace your steps." Having announced the decision to the rest of the party, the leaders started the descent. A figure suddenly loomed up out of the mist, a solo-walker heading uphill. "If you're interested," he said, "there's been an accident back there." All eyes turned to us. "What's happened and where?" I asked quickly. He told us that two men had fallen out of South-East Gully on Great End. One was injured and no rescue team was in attendance. We put on a spurt, following his footsteps down towards where we thought the bottom of the gully might be.

Instinct or luck, we located the casualty within minutes. "What were you doing?" I asked the young man nursing a broken leg. "Practising for the Alps," he replied. They had been using an ice-axe belay in unsuitable snow conditions and had learned a lesson, albeit a painful one. Our Army team unpacked the enormous rucksacks they had been carrying all day and while we dealt with the fracture they produced sleeping-bags, primus-stoves, kettles and mugs. Morale was restored.

Suddenly, we heard shouting above us. Another figure appeared out of the mist. I warned him to move to one side of our casualty. "There's been an accident," he was shouting. "It's okay, were dealing with it." "But you can't be. It's over there." Unbelievably, a second accident had occurred in the neighbouring gully. Leaving our casualty in capable hands, three of us made our way rapidly to the foot of Central Gully. A girl was screaming hysterically, but seemed uninjured. Near to her, her friend lay with severe head injuries and above, a man lay quietly, limbs twisted but obviously conscious. One of the soldiers led the girl away, trying to comfort her, while we sorted out the other injuries. A quick check showed that the man was a spinal casualty, probably suffering irreparable injury and that the girl with the head injuries was the priority.

Speedy decision-making was called for. Our group was unable to evacuate all four casualties unaided, so two were despatched to call out the rescue team. Two more were sent to bring the stretcher from the stretcher box a short distance away. The rest dealt with the first-aid, comfort and safety of the injured. While we waited we discovered what had happened. The three climbers were almost at the top of the gully. They were all roped together and all climbing. They wore no hats. One slipped, pulling the other two. All three fell some seven hundred feet, repeatedly striking exposed boulders and the unprotected crampons of their colleagues, strapped on top of their rucksacks.

The stretcher arrived from the Styhead Box and our unconscious casualty was loaded on. As they moved down towards Seathwaite they met the rescue party on its way up. A quick check confirmed the location and the two groups parted. Despite the speed of the rescue, this girl still faced over an hour's drive to Carlisle. These were the days before helicopters.

The hysterical girl, by now reasonably calm, was deemed to be a walking casualty, although she was later found to have a broken arm. She was escorted well to the rear of this main descent group. The next evacuee was the spinal casualty, who had no pain but was feeling cold. Last to go was the first to fall, who accepted his lot with stoicism. Some five hours after his fall, he was admitted to hospital, full of praise for the care he had received. "Thank goodness the Army got lost," we joked. Their loaded rucksacks certainly saved the day and the lives of four casualties.

A lad missing on Helvellyn

"Mountain rescue is becoming the fastest growing sport in Lakeland," one of the team members commented cynically. "Move into the area and the first thing they want to do is join a team, blue lights flashing, horns blaring, glamour and glory boys." "Yes, but that type doesn't last long," someone else retorted. "To be a rescuer you have to be a bit odd, like." Everyone laughed agreement. After all, who actually enjoys getting out of a warm bed at three in the morning to look for someone who's often not there? "It's just a job that's got to be done by someone," philosophised another. The atmosphere in the pub after the team meeting was relaxed. Men who usually met to perform a common service talked now as individuals. Some were professional mountaineers, guides and instructors. The majority had other jobs but were none the less skilled in mountaincraft, first-aid and rescue techniques. The team attracted a variety of people including shop-assistants, teachers and guest-house owners of varying ages.

The landlord came in to announce a message from the police. A lad was missing on Helvellyn. Pints were hurriedly downed or left and people moved towards the door. Everyone knew what to do. Some drove, some walked to fetch their ready-packed equipment. Long-suffering wives took packets of sandwiches from the deep-freeze and prepared flasks of coffee. Half-an-hour later the first truck-load of men left the town.

The briefing was performed as we travelled along. Two young lads, about fourteen, had left Keswick that morning. They intended to walk along the Helvellyn ridge to Ambleside. One of them turned up at the youth hostel at St. John's-in-the-Vale. He hadn't seen his mate since five o'clock that evening. We pulled into the car-park and groups of two or three set off to cover the specific areas. Searching was something you did on your own. The idea was to know who was to your right, who to your left and how far away they were. The terrain made this difficult, if not impossible. Use of radio in recent years had greatly eased the job. After half-an-hour, my radio crackled a message: "Hang fire lads. I'm getting this bloke out of bed again. He must know where he saw his mate last." I shouted into the

Carrying a mountain stretcher over rocky ground.

The search control radio co-ordinates the search.

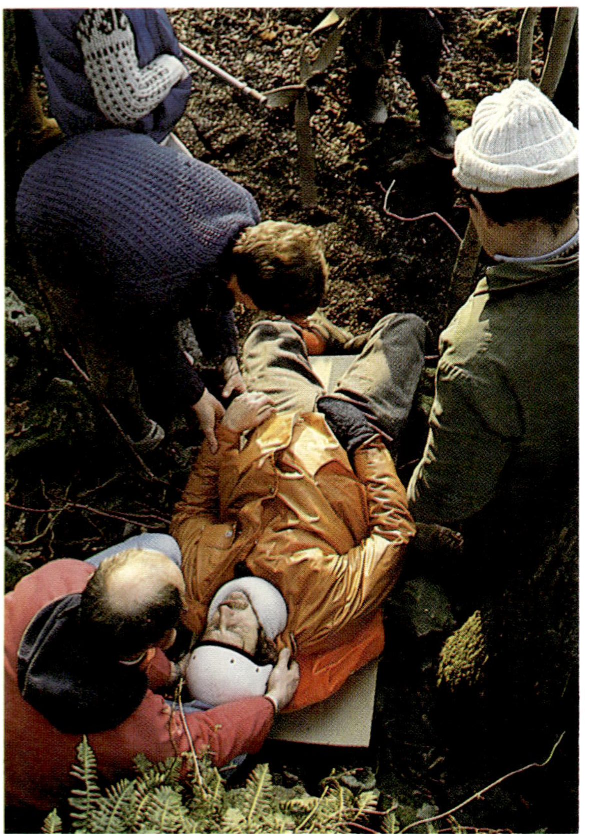

Attending to an injured climber.

Preparing for an unpleasant descent into the mine.

At the foot of the crag.

The miner hauled to safety.

A broken leg, but a cheerful patient!

Roadside first aid for a walker.

44

A difficult location.

Winching up the stretcher.

45

Searchers boarding the helicopter.

Rescue, Skew Ghyll.

Fighting a fell fire.

A fox-hound resisting rescue!

Rescue in an April blizzard.

A search in poor visibility and bad weather.

darkness and received a reply. Three of us moved together and I relayed the message. We sat down in the shelter of some rocks and got out the coffee. The night was silent and still. Only the lights of vehicles in the valley pierced the blackness. Our torches were off, saving the batteries for what could be an all-night affair.

The radio called again into the night. "The missing boy was last seen at nine p.m. above Thirlspot. All teams move into the crags in that area and search from the path down to the fields. Over." We moved into the new search area, commenting on the message. "Seems a bit strange. First he saw him last at five. Now it's nine and he knows where he lost him. You can see the hotel from here or at least the road."

We swept along the crag-line and met at the path, with negative results. We reported back by radio. The reply came clearly. "Do it again. That lad is definitely there." "Well, he must be hiding," said my colleague. "Or dead," I added. "I think there's something ominous about this." We moved, intending to sweep downwards. At about four o'clock, with the dawn just breaking, we heard a shout. "He's here, lads." Hurriedly, we located the caller. The body of the boy was just visible in the early light. He had fallen from the track and was lying face-down in the bracken. "I thought so," I said. "That poor little devil saw him fall, realised he was dead and panicked. What an experience for a kid."

We covered the body and sat silently waiting for permission to move. A rosy light began to spread through the valley, the start of another day. For some the morning would bring sorrow and questioning, but for us our task was done. We were tired, relieved, but not entirely satisfied. An ending like this was not one we relished or cared to dwell on. Best forgotten, by us.

I'm fine, but where are my teeth?

The pleasant Spring morning had driven me to work in the garden. I was busy there when the 'phone rang. "Chap broken his arm on Glaramara," said the policeman. I grabbed my gear and ran down to the rescue headquarters. It was warm enough down in the valley but being immobilised on the tops was another matter. We drove down Borrowdale, collected equipment and set off. A cloud covered the sun. Large flakes of snow started to fall. We cursed our stupidity in not bringing waterproofs. Later, we realised our lack of foresight in not bringing gloves. Bare hands stuck to the metal parts of the stretcher and other equipment. It was intensely cold.

Visibility was down to about four feet and our party had become separated. I carried a radio which told me that some of the team had arrived at the casualty. The location was clarified as the summit of Glaramara. I pressed on, arriving with half a stretcher. "Great, if the casualty's a midget," muttered a friend. The man was with a small group, who had fortunately put him into a survival bag and covered him with warm clothing. Several inches of snow now covered this heap, insulating him. He already had one arm in plaster and had overbalanced on the summit and descended the thirty-foot crag in one large step. "He was unconscious, so we took his teeth out," one of his colleagues told us. "He seems okay now but we think his arm's broken. That makes a pair," they chuckled insensitively. They too were feeling the cold and we suggested that they should start to move down carefully in front of the stretcher party.

By now the whole team had assembled and the patient was prepared for the sledging and carry to the waiting ambulance. We set off into the murk and gloom, checking the casualty from time to time. Each time he confirmed his satisfactory condition gummily. I wondered casually who was carrying his teeth. As we reached the bottom of the fell we came out of the snow-cloud and the whole colourful procession was seen as though the lights had suddenly been switched on in a darkened room. Bright orange and blue clothing contrasted sharply with the sparkling white snow.

As we loaded the casualty into the ambulance I checked his condition again. "I'm fine," he said, "but where are my flaming teeth?" I looked to his companions for an answer. Shamefacedly, they explained, "When we took them out we put them down on a rock and then it snowed. "I'm afraid they're somewhere on the top of that mountain." People find some strange things on the fells, but no report has ever been made of false teeth.

Another dried up dinner

The doctor had become involved with the rescue team when he started practising in the town thirty years before. He was one of the old-timers, would turn out at all times of day and night, thought nothing of walking miles up a mountain-side with his little black bag and never devalued the work done by amateurs such as ourselves. He was respected and loved by all who came into contact with him.

"Do you think we need a drip setting up?" his keen young assistant asked. "No," he replied. "It makes the carry too difficult for the team and the doctors in hospital won't thank us if it pulls out on the way down. Just get him down lads, the best you can. There are two schools of thought in rescue medicine," he elaborated. "One favours going to ground with the casualty and extensive field surgery but I take the view that they have to be got down at some stage and the sooner the better, before the patient starts feeling pain. You're the experts in this game."

As we stretchered the patient down, he escorted us, looking out of place in his suit and shoes but managing remarkably well. "An old lady 'phoned me from miles out last week," he chatted. "It was eleven o'clock at night and she said it was important. I raced all the way there and asked her what was wrong. She said, 'It's not me, Doc, it's the parrot. It's got out of its cage and is stuck up the bedroom chimney.' Well, I had my overalls in the car so I just slipped them on and fetched it down for her. She was very grateful and said, 'Thanks, Doc. I didn't know who to send for.' He chuckled to himself.

"I hope you didn't mind us sending for you, Doc?" said the team leader. We were a bit concerned about him." "Of course not." We'd just finished evening surgery and my young partner here was keen to see what you chaps got up to. I'll go with him to hospital. If one of you could just ring my wife and tell her I'll be a bit late for dinner, I'd be grateful." We marvelled. Nothing was too much trouble for this man. "I took the old ambulanceman down to London to get his O.B.E., last month," continued the doctor. "He'd never been outside the county in his life and he's seventy-six. I thought I'd give him a treat and took him sight-seeing on the Underground. At the end of the day, I turned to him and asked, 'What do you think of London?'

Looking me in the eye, he replied, 'Well, Doc, I think it's not safe. The whole damned place is hollow!' " He eased the difficult carry down with such tales, but nevertheless kept stopping to remind us to check the casualty.

"I see one of the Welsh teams has a doctor who goes out every time with them," I told him. "Is he a mountaineer?" he asked. "I don't know, but he's a doctor." "Not much good if he can't get to his patients, is he?" he replied, "Anyway, what about his patients in the waiting-room? They're his first responsibility. I keep telling you chaps, you're the experts, you have the experience." As we reached the roadside and the waiting ambulance, the radio came to life. Someone was lost. There was the possibility of a night-search. "I wouldn't like your job, chaps," sighed the doctor. "There's always something for you to do. Best of luck. I hope he turns up soon." He climbed into the ambulance with his patient, full of sympathy for us, not thinking that it would be another three hours at least before he would be sitting down to his over-cooked, dried-up dinner, yet again.

Herdwick Broth

The sheep farmer offered to come with us. It was a dark, damp, heavy morning, not very suitable for our first-light search. A small group of us were waiting at the farm at the road-head. It was five a.m., the search due to begin at six. "Come in and look at my fire-place while you're waiting," he said. "I've built it myself from beck cobbles. It's one of them there mineral fire-places." It stretched from floor to ceiling and contained specimens that would have delighted any geologist. "Looks better wet," he said. "Stand clear." He fetched a bucket of water and threw it up the wall. "That's bonny now," he said. We watched the stream of water run towards the carpet and wondered whether his wife would think it looked better wet.

"Right, let's away," he ordered, turning up the collar of his sports jacket. "Are you warm enough like that?" I asked, looking at our array of waterproofs, anoraks, hats and gloves. "Aye, mutton fat in this will turn any amount of rain," he replied. "I'll find you a quick way up. Here Meg, Spot, Fang, here," he whistled and called. The sheep dogs ran up, eager to be off and working. "It's a way up we want, not a sheep-dog trial," we joked. He led at a slow run, until we dropped back to our more normal pace. A fell-runner in his youth, he still showed signs of it, although he said his knees were now full of "screwmatics". A fell-farm is no place for the inactive. Most work was foot-slogging up steep mountain terrain in all weathers, most of them bad.

"See that old lady? She's come down from Sprinkling Tarn," he said. I looked and saw only a Herdwick ewe. "She's a good age now." He recognised all his sheep and we never failed to be astonished at this skill. "They're just like people," he explained, not understanding our puzzlement. "Anyway, who are you looking for?" he asked. "It's a Canadian lad," we told him. "Went up Scafell yesterday, but doesn't know the area. No map, no equipment, no food." The farmer left us, disappearing in the mist.

Ten minutes later, at about two thousand feet, we broke through the cloud layer covering the valley, into the ether clarity of a cold winter morning. Below, the cloud was like solid, grey foam. The peaks pierced it, looking like little islands in the sea. The early-morning sun shone brightly. Everything was silent, the cloud muffling any valley sounds. A figure was clearly seen about a mile away, heading down towards us. "Our Canadian?" we queried. Indeed it was. He had spent a chilly night on the Pike but was none the worse for this experience. He was quite surprised to find that anyone was searching for him. "Your girl-friend was worried," we told him. "Gee, women," he groaned. "Say, you wouldn't have anything to eat, would you?" Within a short space of time he had consumed three men's rations for a whole day.

We moved down to the farm, where a touching reunion with the lonely girl-friend took place. We went inside to sample some home-made broth. "This is good stuff," we complimented the farmer's wife. "Should be, I threw a dead Herdwick into it," she retorted. "I see he's been showing you his mineral fire-place." "Yes, very nice, too," we said. "Aye, new carpets would be nice too. These look like the Borrowdale Flood disaster all over again."

Bank Manager in deep water

The brilliance of the summer morning was not reflected in the gloomy slouching of the policeman up the main street. He was wanting some cheap paint for his boat. "Short of money? Well, if you will buy these expensive toys." "I didn't buy it," he said. "Someone gave it to me. I couldn't afford anything like that." He was always on the cadge, never had enough to make ends meet and said there was "too much on at the nick." I changed the subject. "Anything interesting happening?" "Not really, but there's someone missing in Wasdale."

Later that afternoon the telephone rang. It was a call-out and I ran to the headquarters. The same policeman was crouching down, looking under the tables. "Have you lost something?" I asked. "No, I was just wondering if there was anything going spare." I grinned. "Anyway, what's on?" "A chap has fallen into Blackmoss Pot, if you know where that is. Is it a cave?" "No, it's a very deep pool in the Langstrath Beck. People often jump in to cool down after a fell-walk. Some never come out. It's a lovely spot on a summer's day. Come and see it?" I urged. "No, I have to stay here. That chap's still missing in Wasdale. He might turn up." Yes, but not here; I thought.

We headed down the valley, busy with holiday traffic. We were glad to leave the main road and travel up the track towards Langstrath. This too was crowded, but only with walkers. We left the vehicle at Fairy Glen and after collecting the equipment started to walk up to Blackmoss Pot. "Yoo hoo, over here." A woman waving a white hanky came into view. "We've rescued him. I think he's going to be alright," she bellowed at the top of her voice. "He floated downstream and we were able to pull him out." "How did he get in in the first place?" we asked. "He said he was just standing there and the next thing he knew he had fallen in," she explained. I looked towards the casualty, who was wrapped in everyone's spare clothing. He had turned and was staring at me in a strange way. When I caught his eye, he looked away quickly and seemed to become unconscious. We turned him into a recovery position and put him on a stretcher. I was not convinced that he was unconscious. "Did you get his name?" I asked. "No, he couldn't remember it," she said.

Puzzled, we carried him back to the truck. Once inside, he regained consciousness. "How do you feel?" I asked. "Okay," he answered. "What's your name?" I questioned. He faded out again. We unloaded him at the hospital, but it was not until the next day that the whole story emerged. He was the man missing from Wasdale. He was also a bank manager with financial problems and a potential suicide. Fortunately, he'd changed his mind. When he found himself in Langstrath, he'd waited until he saw some people approaching and then jumped into the Pot. His 'unconsciousness' saved the need for explanations. His half-hearted attempt justified his suicide threat but saved his life. "All's well that ends well," I commented to our policeman friend. "That's as may be," he moaned, "but I had all the paper work to do."

We spent our honeymoon here

I flogged up the ghyll in thick, wet mist. I was walking for the pleasure that hard, physical exercise brings, with no real purpose other than to keep going. I was soaked to the skin and enjoying every minute of it. With no stretcher to carry, no casualty waiting, I felt free. At the head of the ghyll, I climbed out on to the fellside and headed for the tourist track down. The rain had stopped and the cloud was lifting. I was anticipating a quick trot down, a ride home, a hot bath, dry clothes and lunch. Luxury costs little!

As I passed the old coaching inn, I noticed the rescue vehicle parked near the back. I glanced at the clock. It was still only mid-day — late for a search, early for a rescue. I went in to check. A woman and two boys were standing, looking worried. The proprietor came over to me for a quiet word. A few of our lads had gone up the beck. The lady's husband was missing. He had walked up to see the waterfalls about two hours before. He sat down and the kiddies went on up. When they got back, he was nowhere to be seen. The woman came across and spoke: "I'm terribly worried. He wouldn't have gone and left us, there's no question of that. I know something has happened to him. We spent our honeymoon here thirteen years ago, and this is the first time we've been back. He just sat down to wait for the boys to come back and they only left him for about half-an-hour. I just don't understand it. Ever so many people have walked up there looking for him and there's no sign, but I know he must be there." I reassured her, "If he's there we'll find him."

I walked up to join the others. They reported "no sign," though they had been up and down half a dozen times. The track climbed alongside a dozen or so cataracts, some small, some large. "Who's on the other side?" I asked. It appeared that everyone had searched the right bank, where the man had last been seen. With difficulty, I crossed the beck and moved upwards.

In the bottom of the first waterfall, I noticed something pinkish. The colour was not right for a mountain stream. I thought it looked like a drainage pipe. I climbed cautiously down the fifty or so feet of crag into the beck bottom to investigate. The pink object was under the waterfall and just breaking the surface now and then. As I got within twenty feet of it, I saw to my horror it was an ankle. My heart gave a shuddering leap. Unable to reach the body unaided, I climbed out and called to a companion on the opposite bank. He brought a rope and joined me. I quickly tied myself on and left him to belay. I worked along a ledge above the beck and was just able to grasp the man by his collar. We lifted him on to the bank. I felt sick. We looked at each other. His wife would have to be told and the police notified to give permission to move the body. "He must have slipped in from up there on the opposite side," I said. "There's the track." I walked slowly down towards the hotel. The wife came towards me. She sensed the news. "He's dead, isn't he?" she said quietly. "I'm sorry, yes." I put my arm on hers. "I'll have to tell the boys," she said. I left them and contacted the police. The hot bath I'd been looking forward to came much later than planned. I no longer wanted the meal.

A cold and wet Police Inspector

A small group of us stood in the field waiting for the rescue helicopter. In a winter of exceptionally heavy snowfall, the anticipated gully avalanche had finally occurred. Unfortunately, it had happened on a Sunday afternoon in one of the most popular areas of the district. Dozens of climbers and walkers were reported to be in the vicinity, if not involved. Instead of rushing out to perform a traditional-style rescue, we had contacted the Sea King helicopter base on the North-east coast. They were sending an aircraft to airlift the rescuers and equipment to the scene and then to evacuate the casualties. We were surprised and relieved that so little effort was needed on our part and stood chatting and laughing as we waited.

A police van drew up and three officers stepped out. They strode across to us and we were introduced to the new Divisional Superintendent, who was touring his area. Unlike their colleagues in Scotland, the police in England have no statutory duty with regard to mountain rescue, but they are, nevertheless, closely involved and concerned in its workings. "Why not come up with us?" I suggested "and see for yourself what goes on?" "I don't think we're dressed for it," smiled the inspector, looking at his smart uniform. "We're just flying up and flying down," I replied airily. "There's no walking involved." The Superintendent thanked us.

The helicopter came into view, like a large yellow dragon-fly. It landed but we did not move until signalled to do so. The noise and gale from the rotors were terrific. I got out my camera. As I jumped aboard I pointed to the camera and the window. The navigator nodded. Satisfied, I sat at the rear with an excellent view. The rest of the team and the policemen were pointed to seats on either side of the aircraft, unable to see out. The tremendous din from the engines and rotors prevented all communication.

We rose rapidly and set off down the valley. I clicked away happily from my vantage point. Within minutes we were climbing up above the tarn towards the avalanche site. The rotors began to frap and the motion inside the aircraft became unpleasant. We started to lose height. I looked down and saw to my horror the snow-covered tarn immediately below us. I caught the eye of some of my companions, pointed out of the window and mouthed "Tarn." They smiled happily. Trying not to panic, I thought quickly. If I photographed it and we landed on it and sank, they would process my film and discover what went wrong. Such logic! We landed, of course, well clear of the tarn and waited. This was an unscheduled stop. I watched in dismay as the navigator pointed in turn to my colleagues and the policemen and then jerked his thumb out of the door. His meaning was obvious, get out! Puzzled, they complied and jumped out into snow about a foot thick. I tried not to look at the police as they jumped. Guiltily, I sat with another rescuer as the two of us were lifted to the incident scene. The navigator shouted an explanation. We had been overloaded and the wind had been too strong. The only answer was to jettison "unnecessary" weight.

I looked out as we carried on up. The team were leading the way through deep drifts, the paths being obliterated. The police followed, well to the rear, obviously finding the going difficult in their shoes. The avalanche site resembled Blackpool on a busy day. Brightly coloured people were scurrying around in the snow. To our relief we found everyone accounted for and only one patient requiring hospital treatment. He was already ensconced on a stretcher and we merely had to lift him in.

The walking team had arrived as we had the casualty ready for evacuation. The police inspector transfixed me with a look of mixed fury and hatred, unable to speak. His face was blue with cold and purple with exertion. His shoes and trousers were soaked. He and his colleagues jumped aboard. The navigator came across to me. "We've just had an emergency call for help from a neighbouring team of yours. We'll drop this chap off at hospital in Whitehaven and go straight to this second incident. We won't be able to take you down." Alarmed, I glanced at the policemen huddled inside. "That's fine. The police can go with the casualty to hospital." He nodded. As they lifted off I hoped the policemen would think they were going home. At least they were going down, even if that was thirty miles from where they were supposed to be. We moved down, marvelling at the depth of snow. Reaching the farm, we rang for a vehicle to pick us up. The reply came in the affirmative, but that we had better come in disguise, as a policeman with an axe was waiting for us. News travels fast in this area!

Boy left on summit

It was the second day of the seach. As we climbed the long shoulder up into the mist and the cloud, we felt weary. Returning at nightfall and leaving at first light left plenty of time for sleep, but sleep came only fitfully as mind and body relived the events of the day. The youth who was missing had not asked to be brought climbing in the Lake District. Although he had the body of a man, his mind was that of a child. If he were still alive he would be terrified up here alone and in the dark and low cloud. He'd been afraid on the descent and had refused to climb down a rock scramble. The staff, unfeelingly, had left him to follow. He didn't.

After another half-day searching, a group of us met. We only vaguely knew where we were, quite unable to see any landmarks. We sat down and ate our sandwiches. "I don't think he's here at all," said one, who reckoned he had got down and absconded." Another thought him incapable of that: the staff had believed he was genuinely scared.

Something bright in the crevice of a rock attracted my attention. It was a piece of metal from an aircraft, obviously one that had crashed in the last war.

My colleague suggested the two of us should go up there, — more or less where he was last seen. We climbed slowly upwards, the thick mist hampering our route-finding. At one point we stuck on slimy rock. I pushed him and then he pulled me. It was the sort of day when reaching up for a hold meant an armpit full of water. The ground levelled out and my companion stopped. In front of us, someone in waterproofs was sitting on a rock. He turned and we saw it was a boy. "Tim?" asked my companion. "I'm waiting for my teachers," he replied slowly. "They'll be back soon." "We've been sent to look for you. They're a bit worried about you. Are you alright?" I asked. "Yes, but I'm hungry. I must have missed my tea." "You certainly have." We gave him our remaining food which he ate hungrily. We noticed his hands were white and swollen.

We radioed back to base and gave our approximate position. Shortly afterwards, three other rescuers materialised out of the mist, to tell us that a stretcher was on its way. Tim ate and drank phlegmatically all we could provide him with. He slept for most of his stretcher ride down and after spending a night in hospital under observation was discharged none the worse for his experience. We hoped that those in charge of him had found the experience both belittling and beneficial.

Ex-miner

Angry motorists glared from their stationary vehicles as the Rescue Land Rover drove up the centre of the road, sounding its siren. The traffic jam stretched for a mile out of the town. Exhaust fumes, hot sun and lack of progress accounted for the frayed tempers of frustrated tourists. We left them behind and sped along the by-pass, heading for the mountain track.

The track had deteriorated over the years but was still passable with care. Our equipment rattled and clattered against the metal sides of the truck as we bounded along, avoiding the deepest pot-holes and ruts where possible. Talk was impossible and radio contact was intermittent in this valley. A great lurch and decreasing speed told us we were crossing the beck. The truck shuddered to a halt. "End of the line, lads. You'll have to walk from here," shouted the driver. We piled out and started unloading the gear.

The team leader told us a man was trapped down the shaft. We must take plenty of rope and all the climbing equipment. We could return for the stretcher later — it wouldn't be needed for a while. We puffed up the loose scree of the track, the mid-day sun beating down relentlessly. Leaving the track, we headed up the fell-side to a disused shaft some fifteen hundred feet up where two men were standing next to a hole in the ground.

"He's down here," one of them said, in an embarrassed way. The team leader asked what he'd been up to. "We're supposed to be fencing these disused shafts, because they're dangerous. He's an ex-miner and he thought he'd just have a look in. He must have trodden on a rotten timber over one of the old shafts. He seems to be stuck." The leader shook his head slowly and sighed. He cautiously touched the rock edges of the hole. The rotten slate dropped. "I want two people to stop outside the whole time the rest of us are in there," he said firmly. Everyone understood. These old Lakeland workings were notoriously loose and dangerous. Someone had to be left to raise the alarm.

The team lowered themselves in carefully, leaving a small group out in the sunshine. The hole became a tunnel and torchlight revealed old timber props supporting the roof. "Watch those props," snapped the team leader, his voice echoing through the darkness. "Knock those and we're all done for." A short distance down the tunnel another hole appeared in the ground. Freshly splintered wood partly covered the opening through which the unfortunate man had fallen. Torchlight flickered around as the leader looked for anchorages. He barked out his orders: "Ted, put on some waterproofs. We're going to lower you down. Try not to touch the sides. You two, take the other end of the rope right outside the mine and find a decent belay."

An old plank was placed across the shaft, and Ted was slowly lowered into the depths. Silence was maintained and ears strained, listening for sounds from below. Then voices were heard, followed by a shout from Ted. "I've got him. He's just hurt his arm. It's jammed in a cleft and broken his fall."

They were about sixty feet down. The team leader announced the next move. "We're lowering the McInnes stretcher. Get him into it," he shouted down to Ted. The stretcher was lowered, loose rock showering Ted and the casualty as it brushed against the sides of the shaft. We waited, then the shout came. "O.K. we're ready." We heaved and strained and the nylon rope became thinner as it stretched. "They're not moving," said the leader. "Pull again, steadily." At last, the stretcher started to move slowly upwards. We could hear the rock falling inside the hole as the stretcher made contact with the sides. "Hold it there," the leader shouted. He moved towards the shaft and grasped the injured man. With difficulty, he man-handled him out of the shaft and into the tunnel. The casualty was groaning but conscious. We hauled Ted up rapidly. A quick examination revealed the miner's only injury to be to his right arm. "Saved his life," said Ted quietly. "The shaft dropped about another sixty feet below us." We carried him along the tunnel and out into the brilliance of the summer's day blinking after the gloom of the hours inside the mine. He was made comfortable on the stretcher and as we started to move down towards the Land-Rover, the leader turned to the two shaft-fencers. "Do us a favour, lads. Chuck some dynamite in there, then fence it." They nodded silently.

Fire-fighting

We shouldered our beaters and trudged up the fell-side. A smell of wood-smoke came with the breeze as we joked about the cause of the fell-fire. Rumour had it that a wife had nagged at her husband so much that he'd knocked over the Primus stove on which he was making their tea. Spring had been exceptionally dry that year and the heather and bilberry had quickly caught fire. The flames spread rapidly in the light breeze and now, the next day, about nine mountain acres were alight. As we came over the shoulder, the first flames became visible and smoke obliterated the bright sunlight. The whole ridge was blazing. We stopped. The fire, carried by the wind, was moving to our right. To our left the fell-side was blackened, charred and smoking. The sight was depressing, but we stood fascinated.

The fire-officer thanked us for coming. Could we go down-wind and try to stop it there? It was important, he said, that we didn't get cut off. We mustn't let it corner us on a crag, with no way off. It was burning right down to the peat and had really got a hold. He shook his head and he watched with us and told us reinforcements were coming from other brigades later in the day. We trudged to where he indicated and spread out in a line, bordering the fire. It's heat combined with the hot sun forced us back. We raised our beaters and smashed them down heavily onto the burning undergrowth, causing showers of sparks to descend onto our bare arms. Hurriedly, we acquired a safer technique and continued our back breaking efforts for more than an hour, though with seemingly little effect.

"Water," came a shout. Two men appeared carrying a large metal urn. Each of us was rationed to one cup, which we gulped thirstily. Even our throats seemed to burn, and our clothes were covered with tiny holes where the sparks had settled undetected and burned through. Our skin was hot, dry and dirty. The break over, we continued beating until another shout allowed a further pause. "Move down and start clearing the ground. This beating's doing no good." The fire-officer demonstrated, grubbing up handfulls of heather.

"If we create a fire-break it might stop it moving this way." We complied, cutting our hands on the bracken-stalks in our eagerness. The fire burned on. A throbbing sound reached our ears over the crackling of the flames. The yellow Rescue Helicopter appeared and landed where the draught from his rotors would not affect the smoke and flames. The navigator off-loaded extra firemen, sandwiches and orange-juice.

After lunch, we carried on our useless task. A local farmer appeared with his dogs. We were wasting our time, he said it would burn until it was ready to stop. Fell-fires always did. We scowled at him and beat on. At eight in the evening the County fire-chief arrived, ordering all fire-fighters to leave the fell-side. Tired, burned and filthy, we went home for showers, food and bed.

The fire burned on for two more days and then, as the farmer predicted, a change of wind turned it back on itself and it stopped.

Seven casualties

It was a drab and dismal Sunday afternoon as we manoeuvred the Land-Rover out of the garage. The sleet was making cold puddles in the car park and the fells were blanketed in a dirty white cloud. "It looks like a bad one," said the team-leader as we piled into the vehicles. There were said to be seven injured. "Rock-climbing?" I queried. "No, fell-walking," he replied, obviously puzzled. We fell silent, pondering this fact as we rattled on down the valley. Despite the weather, cars were parked at all the usual road-heads. Plenty of people were out walking.

The farmer was waiting for us and pointed up above the farm. "Up there" he said, "Must have been taking the short cut." Wet ground gave way to new snow as we carried up the equipment. We could see the figures above us on the snowy slope. Most were standing silently, waiting as we toiled upwards. The incredible details became apparent the higher we climbed. At least six people appeared hurt, each surrounded by a small group of helpers. Against the snow the picture resembled a battlefield. We moved quickly from group to group trying to assess the most severely injured.

A young girl lay crumpled at the feet of two men. They had tried to resuscitate her. She had been like this for about an hour, perhaps longer. "Is she . . .?" "I'm afraid so. Just stay with her, while we see what else is needed." I said. Her boyfriend lay about fifty feet away from her, with a severe chest injury. He was coughing and in pain. "It was all my fault," he groaned, as I knelt beside him. "I slipped on a patch of ice and she followed to help me." He coughed painfully. "Just let's make you comfortable and then we can get you down." "Is she alright?" he asked. The question dreaded by rescuers received its only answer — the truth. We lifted him onto the stretcher. His pain would, we hoped, prevent him from worrying about the consequences until later. A stretcher with the body of the girl was brought down by a second group.

As I strapped up the wrist of a third casualty, I gently asked him what had happened. It seemed that they had been descending the mountain after a good day's walk. The young man with the chest injury was leading but suddenly hit a patch of ice and disappeared.

The girl had run after him and also fell. Then our spokesman himself had gone to help. "It was just like a skating rink," he said. "All around was fairly soft snow and then there was this patch. The other four fell after me." "Four?" I questioned. "Yes, we all came down," he concluded. I quickly took stock of the situation. We could account for the dead girl, the chest injury, the broken wrist and three with bruises and fright. One person was still missing.

The team leader detailed two of us to search the immediate area, but the seventh casualty was not to be found. We followed the stretcher parties down to the farm to reassemble and reassess the situation. As the ambulances took away the injured we stood together in the farm-yard. The farmer appeared again. "All over?" he called cheerily. "No, we've one missing," I said. "There was a lass brought down by two walkers just after you went up," he said. "But they didn't pass us," we replied. "No, it seems she landed up in yon ghyll," he said. He pointed towards the beck, about quarter of a mile from where we had found the other casualties. "She'd hurt her back," he said. We wondered how on earth they got her down. "Just walked her, like," he replied. We tried not to think of the possible outcome.

As we travelled back up the valley, the snow-covered ground became wet earth. No need for ice-axes down here. This was the problem — getting people to understand that mountain weather was vastly different from lowland weather. But who were we to criticise? Mistakes and accidents can happen to the best-prepared. Some people live to benefit from their own mistakes. Perhaps some live to learn from others. The horror story we had witnessed would not be told until the day of the inquest.

An old lady missing

The eight-year old stood near to tears at my front door. He said his nana had gone wandering again. His dad wondered if we'd help. Of course we would. He had come down here with his brother in his car. I told him to go back and tell his dad we'd be up in half an hour.

I rang around a few of the team members. All quipped cheefully, "Not again?" but they all turned out. The old lady had lived all her life in a cottage in the forest. When her forester husband had died, her daughter moved in with her family to take care of her. The old lady, proud, decided she did not need to be taken care of. Periodically, she would go off walking in the forest, which she knew like the back of her hand. Every track, every lane was etched in her memory like a map. She would forget the year, meal-times, familiar faces, but never did she forget her way.

I jammed the vehicle into second gear and laboured up the steep road through the woods. We stopped at the cottage, where the family were standing disconsolately at the door. The old lady's son-in-law walked across, concern overcoming his embarrassment. "I'm sorry," he said. "She's been missing about two hours. Last night, we locked her in her bedroom because we could see she was ready to go off again. About midnight when my missus went up to check that she was all right she found she had stripped all the wall paper off the walls. Now tonight, this. I just don't know what to do. This time the wife thinks she's really going to . . . well, you know.

We reassured him as best we could and then formed ourselves into small groups, some with search dogs. There was the possibility that the old lady had fallen and injured herself and wasn't just playing hide-and-seek with us. There was also a chance that the family's worst fears might be justified. The whole forest had to be searched, an almost impossible task. Seven of us spaced ourselves along the road ready to do a line-search of a particularly thick plantation. At a signal, we moved forward into dense, unbrashed conifer thicket. Stooping, using hands as much as feet, with twigs catching against any unprotected part of the body, we scrambled along. The theory of this type of search was that the searchers kept in touch with those on their immediate left and right. This then ensured a methodical covering of ground. Of course, in practice this was rarely the case. After an hour, I emerged from the thicket and stood upright on the forest track. No other rescuers were visible or even audible. I wiped grimy sweat and bits of twig from my face and turned left up the track.

The light was beginning to fade, when crackling twigs made me stop. Someone was coming up through the plantation. I stepped behind a tree. No point in frightening her off now, I thought. Another searcher emerged from the thicket and paused to wipe his brow. Disappointed, I stepped out. He had been the end of the search line. Somewhere between us should have been two more men. So much for theory.

"I don't think she'd go through anything like that," he said. I agreed. But if she'd fallen off the path she could be lying in somewhere like that. A figure came walking down the trail towards us. "She's not that way," he said. "I've come off open fell-side." We stood uncertainly and then his radio came to life. Police enquiries had established that the old lady had been seen in another part of the forest altogether. The search was to move into that area. We turned back the way we had come and made for the road.

The Land-Rover picked us up when we were no more than quarter of a mile down the road. We piled in, finding three others and a dog already occupying the back of the vehicle. Two miles on we stopped and thankfully left our cramped positions. "Let's try the old Miners' Trod," I suggested. This time we took torches. Their lights created shadows among the gloom of the trees. Imagination turned these into the figures old ladies. My companion admitted he didn't even know this path existed. It was not much used. Could it be that the old lady knew about it — it came out just below her house.

Ten minutes later, we saw a light through the trees. I turned sharply, hearing a sound. "Thought I heard something," I explained. "Imagination again," rationalised my friend and we walked on towards the house and the lights. A Land-Rover and a police car were standing outside. As we walked up a policeman emerged from the house. "There's soup and sandwiches laid on for you back down at the car-park," he said. "You're to take the truck and pick up some others on the way." Quarter of an hour later, as we were munching sandwiches and drinking soup, the search was called off. The old lady was safe and well at home.

Two nights later, we were called to the forest again. Once more the old lady was missing. "Where had she been last time?" I asked her son-in-law. "She came from the Miner's Trod about ten minutes after you left the house," he explained. "That's where we were," I exclaimed. "I must have heard something after all. It wasn't my imagination." "She said she was hiding because she was frightened," he explained shamefacedly. "I'm terribly sorry to call you lads out again." Our search again proved fruitless, and the old lady turned up after five hours.

Three days later, she went morning walking and we started to search at lunch time. Some team members had work commitments, so there were fewer of us and the team leader decided to enlist the help of a rescue helicopter. As we followed the by-now familiar tracks and trails it made a pleasant change to see where we were going and also some wildlife. Roe deer showed white rumps as they bounded up the fellside and red squirrels chewed cones and branches.

The arrival of the helicopter shattered the peace of the forest. Without any warning, the thunder of engines and throbbing of rotors broke into the tree tops immediately above us. The sound echoed from the surrounding hills and concentrated within the forest depths. Even we were surprised by its ear-piercing intensity. For half an hour it quartered the forest, then the news came over the radio that the old lady was back home. We had certainly flushed her out this time. The big yellow bird seemed to have frightened all concerned. The old lady did not go missing again.

I don't think he's alive

By mistake a group had ended up in an hotel in Borrowdale after a traumatic and wet day's walking in low cloud and snow. They rang the police to say that one of their number had collapsed in Langdale. Having established that the injured man was with two other companions in Langstrath the policeman turned out the rescue team. The Land-Rover bounced and jolted to a halt at the road's end. We piled out, donning heavy waterproofs and collected the usual equipment, stretcher, first-aid kit, stretcher bed and ropes. As the driver jumped out he landed ankle-deep in a pool of water and soft mud. He cursed to himself, reconciling himself to the fact that he would have to get wet at some point in the rescue.

We set off up the track, walking quickly. This was no weather for lying around and we knew our casualty would be cold and wet. After two miles we were hot from our efforts and wet from inside our waterproofs. An uncomfortable dribble found its trickling way down my neck. "Getting wet is the worst part," I panted. "Once you're thoroughly soaked, it doesn't matter. It's the leaking part that's unpleasant."

Two figures in bright orange appeared ahead, moving towards us. "This looks like something," I said as they stopped. The woman spoke. "I don't think he's alive. You'll find him on the track about half a mile on." "Is anyone with him?" I asked. "No," she said. "We're going down. We're staying in Ambleside." "This isn't Langdale," I told her. "It's Borrowdale. When you reach our vehicles they'll give you a lift down to the hotel. The police will need to talk to you." She did not seem to be taking in what was being said and we detailed a team member to escort them down. The events of the day had had a significant effect upon them so that they were unable to think or act clearly.

We found the man as they had described. He wore no waterproof clothing and was saturated. "What a waste of life," someone mused as we silently prepared a stretcher. A dispirited and depressed stretcher party moved back down towards the road ahead.

His mam's fallen in the snow

We shouted at the driver to tell him he'd turned the wrong way and he screeched to a halt. White mist swirled around the Land-Rover. "You were supposed to go right at the last junction. Check up on the radio exactly where they want us." We had received a confused message and no-one quite knew what to expect. We understood that a woman had fallen in snow and was lying injured. Her son had raised the alarm. While the driver tried to establish radio contact with base, two men emerged out of the gloom and mist. One appeared to have severe facial injuries. "Are you alright?" I asked, as they began to pass us. "Yes, fine," he answered. I looked at his companion. "I'm going to give him a lift home. I think he must have fallen. He says he's staying at a holiday cottage in the village." I took him to one side, advising that the casualty should be transferred straight to hospital. His identity was not known. "Would you like to give us your name?" I asked the injured man. "No, I'm alright. I'm staying here," he protested. "Where?" I persisted. "Somewhere here," he replied vaguely. "Well this chap will take you to hospital to have you checked over," I said firmly, looking knowingly at his driver.

As we stopped at the farm the winter's day was already drawing to a close. The farmer came out, having heard our approach. "There's a little boy come down in a panic. Said his mam's fallen in the snow up yonder." He jerked a thumb up into the darkening mist. "I've been up as far as the mine. That's where his footsteps finished." "Was there anyone else with them?" I asked. "Aye, a man," said the farmer. "Don't know what happened to him." "I think we've already found him about a mile away in that direction." I said. "That probably means they were on the ridge. The man fell one side of it and the boy fell the other," I surmised. The farmer offered to put the lad to bed there.

We unloaded ice-axes, crampons, ropes, torches, flares and radios. There was no point in taking a stretcher until we located the woman. We needed two teams to work up each gulley and a stretcher party to wait down here for our call. We set off into the snow and darkness. Out of the village the full force of the wind hit us. Barely

"

able to communicate because of its noise, we made our way slowly, often on all fours. Fresh snow plastered iced becks and the going was difficult.

I heard a call. "Here," it came. "Where are you?" I shouted against the wind. "Shine a light." A light flickered above and to my left and I panted up towards it. My companion shone his torch to where the body of a woman lay on the brink of a waterfall. She was half-covered in fresh snow. I used the radio to notify the others that the search had ended. There was no way we could move her that night. For a start, we didn't really know exactly where we were. We lifted the body to a place of safety and secured her. Then, having marked the location with an orange survival bag and ice-axe, we made our way back down to the farm.

The day after was again one of blizzards and gales. We were not even able to get the vehicle along the road and had to walk a mile in deep snow to reach the farm. However, the daylight at least enabled us to see where we were walking. We pieced together the story as we climbed steadily upwards, pausing often for breath. The man, woman and boy had been descending and were caught out by the storm. They had one ice-axe, which they had given to the boy. The ridge was ice-covered and a short way down from the summit the woman slipped. The man, in rushing to help her, also fell. He had travelled about a thousand feet and suffered a fractured skull, remembering nothing. The woman had fallen about eight-hundred feet and stopped short of a waterfall. Both had disappeared from the boy's sight. He ran and slithered the whole way down to the farm and raised the alarm and he could barely comprehend what had taken place and his grand-parents were travelling up that day to collect him. The descent with the body was both lengthy and hazardous. We were all relieved to get down. As we moved past the farm I glanced up and saw a small boy's white and frightened face at a window. This would be a holiday he would never forget.

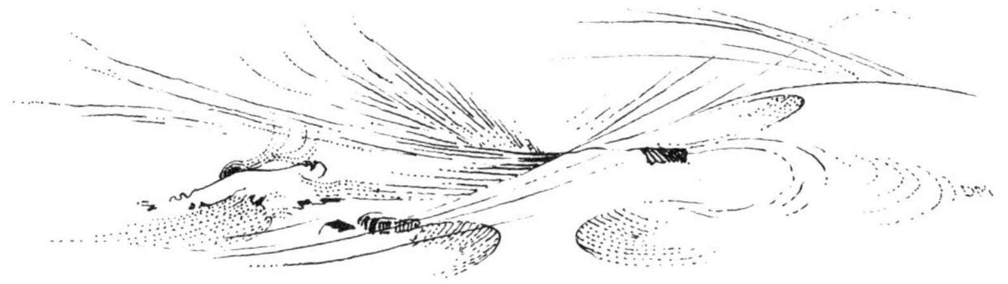

He's dirtied his nappy

A group of us was shown into the interview room. The usually quiet police station was bustling with activity. The Mobile Incidents Control Unit was parked outside and extra officers had been drafted in from surrounding areas. Now they had asked the Rescue Team to become involved. A two-year-old was missing from home. He had disappeared from the garden while his mother was hanging out the washing at eight o'clock in the morning. Now, at ten o'clock she was frantic and a full-scale kidnap enquiry was underway. We were involved because the child lived in a remote part of a hamlet high up on the fell-side in the forest. There was just the chance that he had wandered off into the forest, but as he was only two years old and wearing no shoes and police had already covered the immediate vicinity of the cottage, that wasn't thought likely. The family dog was also missing. Police didn't know if the two were connected. We left the station and headed out of town. It was a fine Spring morning, birds were singing and the sun was shining. "Grand day," someone said. "For some," another added. The police having searched the garden, we started from the boundary fence. The locals had been put in the picture, so they wouldn't mind if we looked through their sheds and out-houses. The team leader speculated that the child wouldn't be far away. "Unless he's been kidnapped," someone said. "There are some funny folk around these days. Time was when you knew everyone you saw." "That" I added, "was when we could leave things lying around too and no-one would touch them. That changed about five years ago. Remember, we left a first aid sack at the crags after a rescue. When we went back someone had taken it. It had a great red cross painted on it as well. Sad."

When we reached the cottage, a small gathering of local people were standing by the gate. They had volunteered to help us search and we split into two's and three's each party going off in a different direction. I followed a grassy field down and turned to watch an enthusiastic band of youngsters as they followed a road that wound steeply up through the forest. "The child's a barefoot two-year-old," I remarked to a companion. "He's not going to go uphill nor use roads, still, I suppose they like to think they're helping."

At lunch-time we stopped and sat down to eat our snack. We travelled about two miles and decided to return to the cottage by a different route. The walking was not too strenuous and the weather pleasant. It was almost enjoyable, were it not for the nagging reminder that our search was for a baby who was missing. By two o'clock we reached the cottage. Search Control was parked outside with telephone lines connected to it. Several police cars blocked the lane and police, searchers and reporters scurried around briskly. A shirt-sleeved officer emerged from the vehicle to pin a type-written statement to the notice-board, but was hurriedly recalled. Ten minutes later he re-emerged to announce: "Call off the search. The boy's turned up." Pandemonium broke out. A grim-faced Inspector walked into the cottage to break the news to the child's mother. We waited patiently. Our job over, we knew that eventually we would know just what had happened. Meanwhile we sat down in the sunshine.

The Inspector returned with the mother and escorted her to a police car. They drove off. Minutes later, a second type-written bulletin was pinned to the notice board. We saw that the boy was safe and well. Police vehicles drove off, Press men scurried down to the telephones and searchers began to return. A smiling policemen came to the Control Room door. We looked at him expectantly. "A local lad found him. He and the dog were three miles away, a thousand feet up in the forest. They've obviously walked, but he can't tell them anything, anyway, the lad won't bring him back. He's dirtied his nappy and lad says it's obviously a job for the police. We've sent his mother." We all laughed, relieved at the happy end to an incredible story.

Search at first light

The phone woke me and, still half-asleep, I picked up the receiver. "Search at first light," came the message. "Right," I replied, stumbling automatically out of bed, dressing and collecting gear and boots. As I reached into the freezer for a pack of sandwiches, I yawned and looked at the clock for the first time. Five o'clock. A glance through the window showed a bright morning with the promise of a hot day. An apple and orange were added to the equipment. It could be a thirsty day's work.

By five-thirty, we were travelling up the valley, having received a quick brief from a tired policeman. We knew that we were looking for a man who had been missing for two days, that he was wearing thick glasses and that he was definitely in the Lake District. "Well, that really narrows it down," someone muttered sarcastically.

Very little was on the move at that time of the morning and we made good progress up Greenup Ghyll. Visibility was good and the sun warm. We enjoyed a pleasant walk up onto the ridge and then paused. Having been in a radio blind-spot until then we were suddenly bombarded by the babble of voices coming over the receiver. Every team in the Lake District was apparently searching for the missing walker. We sat down for a short while as Search Control appealed for radio silence. He gave his position as High White Stones and we glanced up in that direction. "We're supposed to work up to there anyway, aren't we?" my companion asked. I believed so. Picking up our gear, we set off in that direction.

The two controllers were ostensibly in a position which could reach all units operating in the area of search. Even such an extensive one as this. When we reached them, however, three-quarters of an hour later, there seemed to be problems. We found them silent and rather puzzled. "How's it going?" we asked. "We don't know". Apparently everyone had gone quiet all of a sudden. Just then, our radio crackled into life with a message from the team searching Helvellyn. "Hang on" one of the controllers said. "We're not picking up that message on our set. It must be on the blink. That's what's wrong." They took ours as a substitute.

We left them and continued on towards Langdale. The sun was

now high in the sky and we were hot, although not uncomfortably so. Half-an-hour later we came on two other groups from our team and had a quick meeting. An old hand thought the man had come to a sticky end at either Pavey Ark or Pike o' Stickle screes. We tossed a coin to see who went where. All were in agreement — one place seemed as good as another by now.

We won Pavey Ark and headed off in that direction. Halfway down the Rake, I stopped. The scree at the base of the crag was in full view and I scanned it with my binoculars. "What's that?" I asked, passing the glasses to my companion. "Might be something," he agreed, and we moved down to the coloured object on the screes. The body of a man became apparent as we got close the the spot. We tried to raise Search Control and couldn't but Langdale Base intercepted the call and were able to relay the message. We sat and waited, thankful that we didn't have to flog up with the stretcher on such a hot afternoon. Suddenly, a yellow speck appeared above the tarn and the unmistakable sound of a helicopter met our ears. Its noise increased and as it approached, the dust in the scree whirled like a sand-storm. We bent over the body to shelter it and closed our eyes and mouths to keep out the grit. The helicopter landed and the navigator ran towards us with a Neil Robertson stretcher. We strapped the body into the stretcher and ran, keeping low, to the helicopter, lifted him in and then retreated to the rocks. The chopper lifted and was away. Letting the dust settle, we gathered our belongings and headed down to Langdale and a long ride home.

Are you looking for some students

It seemed incredible, eight people missing. "That's what the report says," said the sergeant wearily. "As if we haven't enough problems with roads blocked and people stranded." He outlined the story that he'd been given. A university climbing club had left to walk around the back of Skiddaw to Mungrisdale. The coach-driver had dropped them at Keswick and was to pick them up at Mungrisdale at four p.m. Meanwhile a blizzard had blown up and the group had not appeared.

With the poor visibility and heavy snow, we surmised that the group would have been unable to locate the track to Mungrisdale and would either be stranded at the old shepherd's hut, known as Skiddaw House, or make it down to the road at Dash Falls above Bassenthwaite. We decided to make the long trek into Skiddaw House.

Six of us climbed into the Land-Rover and set off. Even in town the snow was sticking and all traffic was slowed. As we approached Bassenthwaite a post-office van signalled us to slow down. He warned that the road to Dash was absolutely impassable. We decided to try.

We slithered through the village and over the bridge. Once into the wood the road was only dusted with snow and our progress was good but as we rejoined the top road at the cross-roads we were amazed by its condition. Drifts four feet high curled across the road like frozen waves. As far as the eye could see in both directions the road was solid snow from wall to wall. We stopped and got out. As we stood trying to decide which way we should dig, we heard a shout and saw a light being waved down at the farm.

We floundered our way along the farm lane. Snow was still falling, but although the sky was rapidly darkening, the reflection from the snow enabled us to walk without torches. "Are you looking for some students?" the farmer asked. He had just had a phone call from Dash Farm, where they had been found in the barn. They were stopping there until tomorrow. We trudged back to the vehicle and made for home.

The next morning, unable to raise Dash Farm, I rang our farmer friend. "The lines are down to Dash and you can't get through at all. But there's certainly no sign of life from that direction," he said. "We'd better come out, just to make sure. Is Park Wood still open?" I asked. "Just," he replied.

The going was easy along the snow-ploughed main roads but there were only tractor marks through the village and along the Park Wood road. Again we left the vehicle at the cross-roads and started down to the farm. Then we saw small, dark spots moving across the white fields. It was obviously a group of walkers setting out from Dash and walking towards the Bassenthwaite road. "They can't walk out that way," I said. "Better try and head them off. Shout as soon as you're near enough to them. Send them this way."

We hurried as best we could in the often thigh-deep snow. When the figures heard our shouts, they turned and headed across to us. They were the university group and all were in good spirits. When we explained our part in the proceedings, they were very apologetic. Content that they were all safe, we understood when they said, "We didn't foresee the blizzard. It was not forecast and when we were caught out there was nothing we could do but stay put at the first shelter. We're grateful for all your efforts."

All's well that ends well

It was a fine summer's night as I returned from a walk to the lake. Crossing the car-park, I noticed that the lights were on in the Rescue headquarters. "Trouble?" I asked, popping my head around the door. The team-leader frowned, scowled and stared at the map on the wall. "Needle in a hay-stack," he muttered. I shrugged at two colleagues and we waited. At last he sighed. A fourteen-year-old lad had not turned up at the hostel at Thirlmere. He was supposed to be somewhere on Helvellyn, according to his route. "We'll have to do a token search" the team-leader said. "Waste of time the full team turning out until daylight. I want you three to search up this ghyll, cross the ridge and come back down this beck." He swept his finger across six mountain miles in a second.

We drove towards Wythburn. This was the sort of search that we seemed to enjoy in some strange way; a warm night, a good walk and little likelihood of actually finding anything. We travelled light, just taking torches, radios and personal survival items. On such a search, some experience and a lot of luck occasionally met with success. However, the odds against a find were overwhelming. It had been compared to a blind man looking for a tin of beans in Keswick. The three of us set off to cover Helvellyn!

A breeze sprang up as we reached the ridge. We had agreed to rendezvous here and when we were all together sat down in the shelter of a cairn to enjoy a cup of coffee. As usual, only one of us had remembered the flask, so the anticipated cup of coffee became half a cup, gulped hurriedly to enable the one cup to be circulated. Refreshed, we moved on, each taking a solitary route. It was already getting lighter in the east, although it was only half past two. By half-three we could see clearly without lights, and by four we were back on the road-side. "Just nice time," I said. "Back home for breakfast and out again for the day search at six."

Six o'clock saw the three of us joining a dozen more, yawning and stretching at the briefing. We learned that a full-scale search had been launched. All Lakeland teams were involved and a rescue helicopter was travelling from the North-East coast to assist. At ten o'clock, the Search Panel was to be convened. This consisted of a representative from each team and the police. Information was collated and search areas re-allocated.

The sun was hot, and everyone wore shorts. We covered an area similar to the one we had searched the night before. This time, however, we could see where we were walking. From the radio conversations we overheard we knew that more than a hundred men were searching that morning. From time to time the helicopter throbbed over us, airlifting searchers and searching from the air.

At one o'clock, a small group of us gathered on the summit. Had the lad gone home without telling anyone, we wondered. We sat swapping old rescue tales for a while, then the radio broke in. "Pan, all teams, message". We knew this meant something important. Some sort of decision had been made. "All teams, return to base. Acknowledge when requested. Maintain radio silence at other times." We headed down.

A policeman stood near our rescue truck at Wythburn Church. "Where is he?" we asked. "In hospital," he replied, strangely unrelated. "Badly injured?" we persisted. "No, not injured at all. He's ill. Actually, he was admitted last night. A local doctor found him here in the church and had him admitted." "Why didn't he tell anyone?" we puzzled. "He did, . . . er, he told the police," he said. "Well what went wrong?" we asked. "Don't know. Some sort of communication problem, I suppose." The explanation came weakly. Still the weather had been good, we had enjoyed a pleasant walk, and the lad was O.K. What more could we ask?

Stuck in a cleft

"Thirty feet up Greenup?" I queried, registering surprise. The policeman nodded. "That's what the telephone message from headquarters said. Tell the team it's not difficult to get to. He's only thirty feet up Greenup. Anyway, the lad that raised the alarm is waiting for you at the hotel. He'll be able to tell you more." As we journeyed through the valley, I repeated his words to my companions. "Typical," they laughed. "I suppose," said the driver intuitively, "the cadet's on duty at Police Headquarters. It's more likely to be thirty feet up a crag in Greenup."

The boy came out of the hotel as we approached. "He's not hurt" he told us, "he's just stuck." "Was he rock-climbing?" someone asked. "No," replied the boy. "We were just walking over from Grasmere." Unable to piece the story together we followed the boy up Greenup Ghyll.

Puffing his way up, a colleague said how much further this was than thirty feet. After twenty minutes, brisk walking brought us to the foot of Lining Crag. Looking up, we saw the boy stuck in a cleft, thirty feet from the ground. Beneath him was a sheer slab of rock. "How did he get up that?" I marvelled. "He didn't get up it," said the boy. "He's trying to get down it." Light dawned. "Do you mean, he's come from the top?" I asked, looking upwards three hundred feet to the summit of the crag. "Yes," said the boy. "He'd nearly made it when he got stuck there." The team leader changed colour as he rounded on the boy. "But it's a rock-climbing crag. You need ropes and helmets and experience. What was he playing about at?" "Well, he wasn't rock-climbing," said the boy defensively. "We stopped to look at the view from the track at the top. While he was getting his camera out, he knocked his rucksack over the edge. It's got all his belongings in it, so he had to follow it down. We didn't realise the track came down here and we didn't know that the 'sack had come all the way down until he got stuck." The team leader whistled through closed teeth and shook his head.

Four of us climbed up the track to the top of the crag and arranged the anchorages. The leader clipped into the rope and lowered himself cautiously down the crag. A second rope was taken down by the leader and, when he reached the trapped boy, he tied him on to it. Then he securely fastened a helmet to his head and signalled for him to be lowered to the ground.

As the boy's feet touched the ground, he slowly crumpled to a sitting position. He was trembling violently and had obviously been more shaken by the whole episode than he realised. Shortly afterwards, however, he had recovered sufficiently to enquire about his rucksack. His friend brought it across and they checked its contents. Unbelievably, nothing was damaged. The leader looked at the boy and at the crag. "Which way did you come down?" he asked. "Not the right way," said the boy. After a short rest, we accompanied the two boys down the valley and gave them a lift to their hostel. We understood that they slept very soundly that night.

Volunteers to the rescue

We had been anticipating trouble all day. It was a Sunday afternoon in early January. Heavy snow had been falling on the tops and white puffs of cloud covered the summits. In the valley, however, it was merely dull and cold. Judging by the number of cars parked in the valleys there were plenty of walkers out and about. The call came at about three p.m. Our team were asked to assist a neighbouring team who, it seemed, were trying to deal with several incidents simultaneously. This is the usual procedure. We learned later that nine separate accidents had occurred at the same time. All the Lake District teams were involved.

At the Traveller's Rest in Grasmere, some confusion was in evidence. A young policeman seemed to be in charge. "We want as many people as possible up to the tarn," he was saying. "What equipment do we need?" we tried to ask. "I don't know", he shouted. "I've just been told to get as many people as possible up to the tarn." Shrugging our shoulders, we took a stretcher, rope and basic equipment and set off up the track.

Twenty minutes later, I was aware of a change in the atmosphere. Lifting my eyes from the ground, I could see snow coming. Ahead of me only one team member was visible. He too was looking around and seeing me close behind, he waited. "That looks nasty," I said. He agreed and we looked around for others. There was a girl some distance below and behind us. We decided to wait for her. Three was better than two in the conditions that we realised would soon hit us.

We hadn't long to wait. Within minutes the full force of the blizzard arrived. We were blinded by the swirling snow as it stuck to our eye lashes. The wind gusted strongly, alternately pushing us along and impeding our progress. Backs bent, we pressed on, the girl finding the going difficult. During the times when we were able to speak, we were gradually able to piece together her story. She had been walking past the Traveller's Rest when she'd heard the policeman shouting about an accident and asking people to go up to the tarn. She had felt obliged to volunteer her help. As she was now finding it difficult to continue and the job clearly beyond her capabilities, we tactfully suggested it might be better if she returned to the valley. Eventually she was forced to agree and reluctantly began to retrace her steps. The two of us plodded on and reached the col. The snow stopped falling as suddenly as it had started. Several groups were visible in the vicinity of the tarn. We joined one with a radio to await instructions. We learned that four walkers had fallen about a thousand feet from Fairfield and we hurried across to where we thought they might be. More people arrived to help and soon each casualty had a small band of rescuers. One man was beyond help. His body was taken down. A young child who had fallen with him was virtually uninjured, despite having fallen the same distance. He was carried down, bruised and badly frightened. A third man had a fractured thigh, which was splinted before he was taken down to Patterdale. Our casualty had a severe chest injury and as he was lying nearer the Grasmere side of the mountain, we decided to evacuate him that way.

By now, most stretchers were in use and we found ourselves forced to wait for one which we were told was on its way. We made the man as comfortable as possible and tried to reassure him. As we waited we became conscious of the fading light. A party of instructors and students from an outdoor pursuits centre arrived with the stretcher. Fortunately, they also had ropes and as they had been climbing, ice-axes and crampons. Such had been our rapid and unprepared ascent that we had none.

Having secured the casualty, we started on the short uphill stretch to reach the Raise Beck track. With volunteers, the carry was far from easy, but we were grateful for their equipment and assistance, without which we could have undertaken nothing. In the beck on the descent, the only way to stay upright was by holding on to the stretcher. This was impossible when we hit ice under the snow and we landed flat on our backs. Although we couldn't see the ice in the dark, we found that this was an infallible means of detecting it! I picked myself up for the umpteenth time, calling to the volunteers to watch their step!

It took over an hour to make our painstaking way down to the road. Throughout, we had talked to the casualty who repeatedly thanked us. Quite suddenly, we turned a corner and found ourselves able to sledge rather than carry the stretcher. Below and to our left we could see headlights and a blue flashing light. We made that way, telling the casualty that he was nearly down and would soon be more comfortable. "I'm fine, I'm fine," he coughed.

We reached the waiting ambulance and handed over to the crew.

We heard later that the man was discharged quite fit some weeks after. While we waited for our transport we collected together the equipment and thanked the volunteers, without whom no rescue could have taken place. A short time later, wet and tired, we were drinking hot soup in Grasmere. I looked at the personal equipment I had taken with me and realised its hopeless inadequacy. To my permanent kit I added a very small torch and a pair of instep crampons. Even rescuers learn something after each rescue.

It's not mine

The dog began to howl pitifully and then curled itself up into a ball, the snow settling on its fur making it look like a husky. We too were fairly cold, despite the fact that we were wearing down clothing and waterproofs. We stomped our feet and tried to keep our bodies moving, although our job demanded that we stayed in one location out in the open. We were search control on a summit ridge. A man was missing in the area and several teams were out searching. It was our job to co-ordinate their activities and relay messages between them and their bases.

The wind was gusting at about force seven or eight, a blizzard was raging and early winter darkness was falling. We had to shout into the radio for our voices to carry above the noise of the wind. Hearing messages was just as difficult. I was attempting to revive my hands and feet when we intercepted a faint message saying that the man had turned up safe and well at his home out of the Lake District. Too cold and uncomfortable even to comment, we quickly relayed the message to all teams and prepared to evacuate. A second transmission came over the radio. "Drop in. The kettles on." Warmed by this cheerful message, we waited for the dog to shake off its covering of snow and hastily descended to the valley.

The receptionist looked up as we walked into the hotel, having removed our boots and wet outer clothing. "He's in the little lounge," she said, quite unconcerned about our unguestlike appearance. Mine host was seated behind the bar. As we entered, he filled two glasses, smiling. "Be a bit nippy up there?" he said. We sat down and started the long night's yarns. Living, as he did, at the foot of some of the most popular rock-climbs in the district, he was naturally the centre of rescue activities. Guests at the hotel would leave a good meal and warm room to follow this magnetic personality whenever he needed help. Such was the warmth of his hospitality afterwards that people gave whatever he asked.

Some hours later, I was surprised to notice that the level of beer in my glass had not appeared to fall, despite my having consumed liberal mounts. It took some time to detect our friend's movements. Each time two or three mouthfuls were taken, he skilully slid the glass under the pumps and refilled it. His actions were barely detectable and conversation was maintained throughout.

Some years later, he retired and moved out of the valley. We visited him to take him an old discarded climbing rope that he needed. His wife greeted us. "He's up in the wood," she pointed. We climbed up the steep bank and found him felling a small ash tree. "How do?" he called. "A rope, just what we need. We're trying to get this ash out of the way and then we can cut down the one behind it." We helped him to tie the rope to the trunk and we all heaved. Slowly, it began to move. Half an hour later, having struggled to bring it down to his timber-pile, we went in for the every-ready coffee. "You're lucky to have your own wood," I said enviously. "Oh, it's not mine," he beamed. "But thanks for your help. Have some more coffee."

Heart attack

I'd been called from work and when I arrived at the Rescue Headquarters I'd already missed the vehicle. I jumped back into my car and made my own way up the valley. The call had come from a farmhouse and I travelled there. A group of villagers were gathered around the gate as I parked in the lane near to the police van and ambulance. One of the locals pointed and said quietly, "They're over there." As I set off across the fields, I puzzled. Strange that all the local people were out. They were not usually interested in rescue activities. Funny time for a rescue too, mid-morning, mid-week. I came suddenly upon the stretcher party descending silently. This too was unusual. Often, when bringing down a body, the rescuers compensated with light chatter and laughter. Someone handed me a carrying strap and I took my turn.

The local doctor came alongside. He was wearing a suit and shoes and looked uncomfortable hot and dishevelled. "Well, just look at that view!" he said. "And what a lovely day. What more could a man want in his last moments. Out caring for his beasts and sudden death, no pain." Everything settled into place. This was the farmer. It was his family waiting down at the farm. He'd had a heart attack while out feeding the sheep.

"Do the family know?" I asked, as we approached the farm. "I think they suspect," said the doctor. "You take him through that field to the ambulance and I'll go and see his wife." Yes, I thought. Sudden death is painless for the deceased, but painful for relatives.

That evening, the family sat quietly in the farm kitchen, trying to console each other. Outside, the farmer's work was undertaken by his fellow-farmers and friends. In such a community, loss and grief are shared. After completing their own work each lent a hand to do the dead man's chores. Livestock needed immediate attention. They would continue in this way until the bereaved wife was over the worst and had adjusted to her new life.

He was seventy three

The constable was having trouble. He couldn't "raise" anyone, he complained to me on the phone. I could give him the reason: a united team practice at Ennerdale. Most of the lads and several other teams were there. "There's a climber unconscious on Black Crag," he said, relieved that at least he'd found me.

Recognising an emergency, I ran down to headquarters. Unconscious casualties were the ones that well-meaning friends often finished off by leaving them lying on their backs. By the time I'd backed the Land-Rover out of the garage, two colleagues had joined me. "We'll drive through town and pick up any useful volunteers," I said. "We haven't time to wait. This bloke's unconscious." Our drive through town increased our numbers to four. A colleague had emerged from his bar lunch on hearing our siren. We set off for the plateau at the top of the crag, each carrying double lots of equipment. It was short, sharp pull and as we went up through the wood I heard our latest companion laughing behind us. "What's up," I panted. "I'm going into hospital tomorrow," he chuckled. "Got to have a hernia operation. The doctor's forbidden me to lift any heavy weights."

At the top of the crag, several groups of climbers were gathered, aware of the drama being enacted on the crag below. We were soon put in the picture. The man had been leading the climb, one he'd done many times before. As he reached the top, he slipped and banged his head, becoming unconscious. His runners had held and he was hanging in his harness. His wife and second had quickly climbed up to him and had been maintaining his airway while balanced precariously on a small foothold. She had been there twenty minutes already. A National Park Ranger known to us had just climbed down to assist.

Hurriedly, we put together the two halves of the split stretcher and lowered it down to the Ranger. He and the wife were able to secure the unconscious man to it. Then, using some twenty volunteers at the top of the crag, we hauled up the injured man.

At that moment, a Sea King helicopter throbbed into view. Realising we were short-handed the police had asked for its assistance. It had been on manoeuvres with the teams at Ennerdale. The navigator was lowered on the winch and was able to assess the situation. The helicopter then returned, dropped a three-hundred foot wire and the navigator attached himself and the stretcher. Slowly, they were winched up and off to hospital.

Just then, the climber's wife climbed out at the top of the crag. She took off her helmet and revealed a mop of grey hair. Surprised, I asked for her husband's details. "He's seventy-three years of age, but please don't put that in the Press. Everyone will say he's too old to be climbing. He's climbed all his life and done that route at least a dozen times. He's never had an accident in sixty years' climbing. Is he going to be alright?" I reassured her on all counts. "Accidents happen to all of us," I said. "It could just as easily have been one of us." The climber spent some weeks in hospital and then was discharged as fit. Unfortunately, he was never able to climb again.

Surly attitude

The telephone bell jerked me from my sleep and I opened my eyes to a bright summer's morning. It was four o'clock and the policeman on duty at the station seemed annoyed at all the extra work at such an early hour. "Don't go back to sleep," he growled. "I'm off duty at six and I want this lot tied up before then."

No-one went back to sleep, because by four-thirty we were on our way to a remote area on the fringe of the North-Eastern fells. "What's happened at this time of morning in a spot like that?" someone asked sleepily. The team leader explained that the police had received a call from a man who told them he was one of a group from the Midlands on a marathon walk. One of the group had collapsed on their first ascent. The informant was supposed to be waiting at the telephone box, but no-one had answered when he had been called back.

Sure enough, when we stopped at the kiosk, no-one was in sight. "Better start up the track then," said the leader, sighing. We set off at a steady pace, carrying the usual equipment. After quarter of an hour, figures appeared above us on the track. As they drew near we saw that this was a stretcher party. The "stretcher" was a gate, and the man lying on it was obviously dead. The group put down their burden. A few of us transferred the man to our stretcher and covered him over.

The spokesman for the group moved towards us. "I called you out," he said. "I'm sorry I had to leave the phone but I wanted to know what was going on. His name and address are on this paper. He's a doctor and a walking friend of ours. We'd just set off and almost completed our first ascent when he collapsed and died instantly. We thought it would save you a long, unnecessary walk if we carried him down. We borrowed the farmer's gate, but we'll replace it when we go back. We've decided to carry on with the marathon. It's what he would have wanted. He was a great walker." He turned and having thanked us, he and his party picked up the gate and left.

We sledged the stretcher down towards the road. It was still only about half-past-five. As we were out of radio contact with our base, I telephoned a message to the police station. Our grumpy friend was still on duty. "The mortuary key?" he moaned. "Not more paperwork? I'll never get finished."

At exactly six o'clock, we pulled up outside the mortuary. The policeman was looking at his watch. Hurriedly, he pushed the key into the padlock, turned it and snapped it off inside the lock. "That's all I need," he grumbled. "I'll have to go and get a hacksaw and cut it off." "Take your time?" we smiled. "We're not in any hurry, neither is our casualty. Anyway, it's such a grand morning. Would have been a pity to waste it sleeping."

Rescuers are not great ones for philosophising about rescues. They see that they have a job to do and they get on with it. However, on this occasion we were all struck by the policeman's surly attitude. We looked at the body of a comparatively young man who'd suffered an untimely death. We thought about the care and consideration of his friends. We thought about ourselves, leaving warm beds in the early hours of the morning. We contrasted these actions with those of the policeman, who was, after all, performing his paid duty. The team leader shook his head slowly and summed it all up: "You're a long time dead."

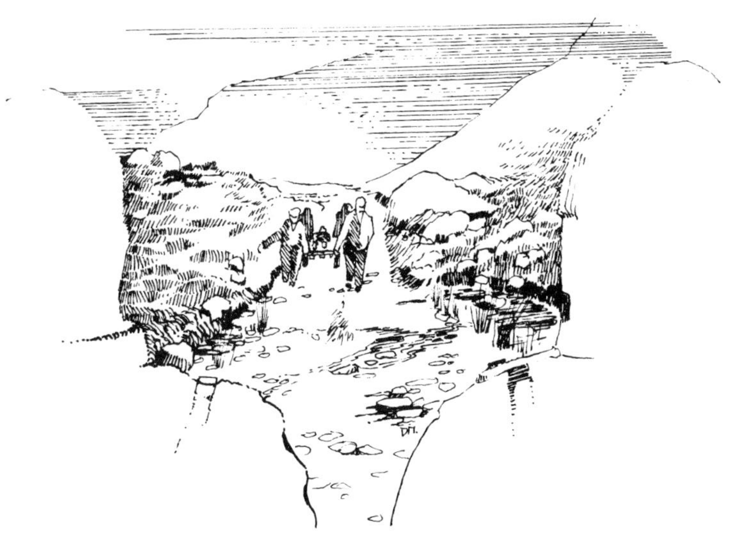